First published in 2006 by New Holland Publishers (UK) Ltd
London • Cape Town • Sydney • Auckland
Garfield House, 86–88 Edgware Road, London W2 2EA, United Kingdom
www.newhollandpublishers.com
80 McKenzie Street, Cape Town 8001, South Africa
14 Aquatic Drive, Frenchs Forest, NSW 2086, Australia
218 Lake Road, Northcote, Auckland
Copyright © 2006 text AG&G Books
The right of David Squire to be identified as author of this work has been asserted by him in
accordance with the Copyright, Designs and Patents Act 1988.
Copyright © 2006 illustrations and photographs New Holland Publishers (UK) Ltd
Copyright © 2006 New Holland Publishers (UK) Ltd
ISBN 1 84537 105 4
10 9 8 7 6 5 4 3 2 1

Editorial Direction: Rosemary Wilkinson Senior Editor: Clare Hubbard Production: Hazel Kirkman
Designed and created for New Holland by AG&G Books Copyright © 2004 "Specialist" AG&G Books
Design: Glyn Bridgewater Illustrations: Dawn Brend, Gill Bridgewater and Ann Winterbotham
Editor: Alison Copland Photographs: see page 80
Reproduction by Pica Digital Pte Ltd, Singapore
Printed and bound in Malaysia by Times Offset (M) Sdn. Bhd.
The information in this book is true and complete to the best of our knowledge. All recommendations
are made without guarantee on the part of the authors and the publishers. The authors and publishers
disclaim any liability for damages or injury resulting from the use of this information.

The CLIMBING PLANTS Specialist

The essential guide to choosing, planting, improving and caring for climbing plants and wall shrubs

David Squire

Series editors: A. & G. Bridgewater

Contents

Author's foreword **2**

Author's foreword

Climbers and wall shrubs are nature's contribution to 'vertical' gardening. They are versatile plants; while some are vigorous and clamber into tall trees, others are more reserved and clothe trellises and walls, as well as growing in containers. Many climbers and wall shrubs produce beautiful flowers, while others have attractive leaves. Some of these are variegated, while a few become drenched in striking colours before they fall in autumn. There are also berried shrubs, and many are extremely hardy and ideal for planting against cold and exposed walls.

Climbing and rambling roses are also featured in this colourful book; many of them have rich and varied fragrances, including, among many others, apple, raspberry, orange, musk, cloves and myrrh.

This inspirational, practical and information-packed book describes a wide range of climbers and wall shrubs, as well as giving vital information about their selection, planting and care.

Making the right decision about which climber to buy and plant is a major part of successfully clothing a wall or trellis. If, after a few years, a climber or wall shrub proves to be too vigorous – or even insufficiently clothing an arch or trellis – it will cause disappointment. This book is therefore an invaluable aid to successful 'vertical' gardening and an inspirational part of your gardening library.

SEASONS

Throughout this book, advice is given about the best times to look after climbers and wall shrubs, as well as the time of the year when they flower or, perhaps, produce berries. Because of global and even regional variations in climate and temperatures, the four main seasons have been used, with each subdivided into 'early', 'mid-' and 'late' – for example, early spring, mid-spring and late spring. These 12 divisions of the year can be applied to the approximate calendar months in your local area, if you find this helps.

Measurements

Both metric and imperial measurements are given in this book – for example, 1.8 m (6 ft).

Climbers and wall shrubs

There is a huge range of climbers and wall shrubs that can provide eye-catching colour in a garden. Apart from their clothing and screening abilities – whether cloaking low or high walls, or dressing pergolas and arches – some, such as a few large-leaved Ivies, are ideal for smothering the ground in colour. Climbers range from annuals and herbaceous perennials to more permanent woody plants. Some are evergreen, others deciduous.

Why use these plants?

WHAT IS A CLIMBER?

Woody and perennial Many climbers are woody, perennial plants, and once bought and planted become permanent features in a garden.

Evergreen climbers Evergreen climbers retain their leaves throughout the year, regularly shedding some and growing fresh ones – but always appearing 'ever-green'.

Deciduous climbers Deciduous climbers lose their leaves in autumn or early winter and develop a fresh array of them in spring, when they are especially attractive.

Annual climbers A few climbers are annuals. These are raised from seeds sown in spring (either in a greenhouse or directly into their flowering positions). They then grow, flower and die during the same season.

Herbaceous climbers Only a few climbers are 'herbaceous', meaning that all of the leaves and stems die down to soil level in autumn, and the plant produces fresh stems and leaves in the following spring.

WHAT IS A WALL SHRUB?

Woody and perennial
Wall shrubs are woody and perennial, and once planted remain part of a garden for many years. Some can also be grown in borders, but when planted against a wall make full use of space and are perfect for small gardens.

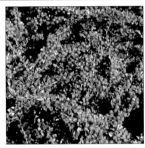
Berried wall shrubs provide an alternative decorative option for clothing walls.

Evergreen wall shrubs Evergreen wall shrubs retain leaves throughout the year, shedding some but continually producing new ones. In cold areas, a few wall shrubs may wholly or partly lose their leaves.

Deciduous wall shrubs Deciduous wall shrubs lose their leaves in autumn and produce a fresh array in spring.

WHAT CAN WALL SHRUBS DO FOR A GARDEN?

Wall shrubs are superb for clothing walls with colourful leaves and flowers; some also have attractive berries which, for some of them, last through to late winter. A few of them are ideal for clothing a wall where there is only a small space between the wall and path.

ROSES

What is a climbing rose? Climbing roses have larger flowers than rambling types, and are borne singly or in small groups and often with the ability to repeat flowering after their first period of bloom.

What is a rambling rose? Rambling roses, or ramblers, bear many large bunches of small flowers. Flowering is usually only for a single period in the year, but they still have plenty of eye appeal.

What is a pillar rose? Many climbing roses can be used to clothe pillars, which are usually rustic posts, 2.1–2.4 m (7–8 ft) high, and often cut from conifers. Alternatively, tripods formed of planed wood can be used.

Tripods generously clothed with roses create dramatic head-height features in gardens.

Range of climbers

Is there a wide choice of plants?

Many climbers and wall shrubs will enrich your garden, whatever its size and orientation. Some of these adaptable and versatile plants have a wealth of magnificent flowers, others distinctively variegated or single-coloured leaves, while some have foliage that in autumn assumes rich and vibrant colours. Other plants have colourful berries or attractive seedheads that bring extra colour to autumn and early winter; some berries persist throughout winter.

QUALITIES TO LOOK FOR

As well as selecting a climber or wall shrub with plenty of eye appeal, there are other considerations.
- Select a plant that will not quickly outgrow its position and swamp its neighbours. In the A–Z of Climbers and Wall Shrubs (see pages 24–39) the approximate height and spread of each plant is indicated; but remember that climbers are adaptable and, if given sideways space, may use that rather than climbing.

- Always buy good-quality, correctly labelled and pest- and disease-free plants (see pages 10–11 for buying plants, and 76–77 for pests and diseases).
- Check the type of support needed. Some climbers are self-supporting, while others need a framework over which they can scramble. Some of these versatile plants are able to clamber into trees or smother old tree stumps. For details of climbing methods, see pages 12–13.

Flowers

Colourful flowers always gain attention and, while some climbers such as *Clematis montana* have masses of individual flowers, others are borne in clusters; few are as spectacular as those of wisteria, with their pendulous nature. Many flowers are fragrant and several are described on pages 58–59. See pages 60–61 for scented roses.

Leaves

The choice of climbers with colourful leaves is wide and encompasses single-coloured types, such as the herbaceous *Humulus lupulus* 'Aureus' which each year produces a fresh array of leaves. The hardy and deciduous *Jasminum officinale* 'Aureum' has leaves blotched creamy-yellow, with the bonus of white, fragrant flowers during mid-summer.

Variegated leaves

Climbers with variegated foliage always capture attention. Some have boldly coloured leaves that clothe walls with colour. Others, such as *Lonicera japonica* 'Aureoreticulata', have green leaves, gloriously highlighted with yellow along their veins. Some climbers also have the ability to smother the ground in handsome colours (see pages 34–35).

Many species of clematis, as well as large-flowered types, are ideal for small gardens, and with their wide colour range will satisfy all tastes (see pages 26–28 for examples).

Humulus lupulus *'Aureus' (Golden-leaved Hop) is herbaceous, with five-lobed, coarsely tooth-edged, bright yellowish-green leaves. They create an attractive screen.*

The variegated Hedera colchica *'Sulphur Heart' soon creates a handsome screen. It is also ideal for planting as ground cover in dappled and light shade.*

GREET COMBINATIONS

CONTRAST	HARMONY

Climbers and wall shrubs can be further enhanced by growing them against colour-contrasting walls. For example, a white wall is ideal for highlighting red, scarlet or yellow flowers. Colours for positioning against grey stone and red-brick walls are detailed on page 62. Background-enhancing your climber is well worth attempting.

Harmonies with flowers, leaves and berries are best achieved by grouping them together. Creating attractive associations with climbers and wall shrubs – as well as climbing and rambling roses – are suggested and illustrated on pages 62–67. These plant associations are simple to create, but magical in their results.

ARE ALL CLIMBERS HARDY?

Many climbers are tolerant of winter frost, as well as flourishing in hot summer weather. Evergreen climbers such as Ivies are exceptionally hardy; many deciduous types are also hardy. The hardiness of each climber is detailed in the comprehensive, well-illustrated A–Z section (pages 24–47).

ARE ALL WALL SHRUBS HARDY?

Wall shrubs have a wide range of hardiness, from the frost-tender *Abutilon megapotamicum* to the winter-resilient *Pyracantha* spp. (Firethorns) and *Cotoneaster horizontalis* (Fishbone Cotoneaster). Before choosing a wall shrub, check with the A–Z section (pages 24–47). Never risk putting a tender shrub against a cold wall.

Autumn colour

Autumn coloured leaves are just as vibrant and eye-catching as summer flowers. Many trees and shrubs are noted for their autumn colours, but few can surpass climbers such as *Parthenocissus quinquefolia* (Virginia Creeper; often known as American Ivy and Five-leaved Ivy). There are many others – see pages 36–37.

Berries

A few climbers have attractive berries, but they are inevitably surpassed by those produced by wall shrubs such as *Pyracantha* spp. (Firethorns) and *Cotoneaster horizontalis* (Fishbone or Rock Cotoneaster). There are both red- and yellow-berried forms of *Pyracantha*; finding the right background colour is described on page 62.

Seedheads

Many flowering climbers later produce attractive seedheads which create memorable displays; some continue well into winter and are especially attractive when covered by frost. Several clematis produce beautiful seedheads, and perhaps one of the best-known types is *Clematis vitalba* (Old Man's Beard or Traveller's Joy; see page 39).

Parthenocissus quinquefolia *(Virginia Creeper) is a vigorous, deciduous climber with brilliant scarlet and orange leaves in autumn. It is visually dramatic.*

Cotoneaster horizontalis *(Fishbone Cotoneaster) is ideal for covering walls with small, glossy-green leaves, as well as berries. It will brighten walls in winter.*

Clematis vitalba *(Old Man's Beard or Traveller's Joy) is a sprawling, cottage-garden-type climber with glistening, silky seedheads in autumn and into winter.*

Climbers for all places

How can I use these plants?

Uses for climbers and wall shrubs range from clothing walls and fences with flowers and colourful leaves to smothering arbours, pergolas and arches in colour. A few climbers can be encouraged to form hedges, clothe old tree stumps and climb into trees. Climbing and rambling roses also have many uses, including clambering over pergolas, covering tripods and pillars and growing into trees. They are often used to cover walls, in either cold or sunny situations.

HOW AND WHERE TO USE CLIMBERS

Climbers are versatile and can be used in many ways. Here are a few ideas on how they can enhance your garden, whether they are clothing walls or, when clambering over a free-standing trellis, creating a screen that blocks off neighbouring gardens or cloaks unsightly features in your own garden, such as dustbins (garbage bins) or fuel-storage tanks.

Clothing walls
↘ Both flowering and coloured-leaved climbers will clothe walls. Some climbers are self-supporting, but others need a wall-secured trellis (see pages 12–13 for climbing methods).

Pergolas
↘ Pergolas – whether of a rustic or formal nature – are ideal homes for climbers, especially those such as wisteria with long bunches of fragrant flowers (see page 50).

Arches
↘ Arches – whether dainty and formed of metal hoops, or informal and constructed of rustic poles – create superb homes for flowering and leafy climbers (see page 51).

Free-standing screens

↗ Square or diamond-shaped trellis panels secured to a series of vertical posts about 1.8 m (6 ft) apart soon create a peep-proof screen when clothed in leaves (see page 53).

Into trees
↘ Several vigorous flowering climbers can be planted to clamber into deciduous trees, where they become distinctive features that invariably capture attention (see page 54).

Tree stumps
↘ After cutting back an old tree, digging out the roots is laborious work. Instead, plant a climber that will clothe the trunk and create an attractive feature (see page 54).

Arbours
↘ Secluded arbours, clothed in fragrant flowers, add distinctive features to gardens. Ensure that a seat or bench for two is fitted into the arbour (see page 52).

Hedges

↗ A few climbers – whether on their own, in partnership with a shrub or intertwined with a wrought-iron fence – create an attractive and unusual hedge (see page 72).

HOW AND WHERE TO USE WALL SHRUBS

Many shrubs can be grown against walls, but with all of them it is essential to have a framework of tiered wires or a trellis to support them. During their early years, many wall shrubs do not appear to need support, but later – and perhaps when they are weighed down by a heavy fall of snow – a supporting framework is essential.

Walls

↑ Many shrubs are ideal for planting against a wall, where tender types gain both wind protection and a sun-drenched position. Cold walls can also be clothed (see page 48).

Screens

↑ In the same way that climbers can create free-standing screens, so too can wall shrubs. In cold areas, however, only frost-hardy ones can be used (see page 53).

HOW AND WHERE TO USE CLIMBING AND RAMBLING ROSES

Climbing and rambling roses do not create such a dense array of foliage as that produced by many climbers and wall shrubs, but they make up for this with their superb flowers.

There are many ways to use roses in gardens, from covering walls and pergolas to adorning tripods and pillars. Many are ideal for covering tall tree trunks or climbing into trees.

Walls

↗ Roses have long been grown against walls, where they create a feast of summer colour. In general, climbers are better than ramblers against walls (see page 48).

Tripods and pillars

↙ ↘ Both climbing and rambling roses can be planted to climb tripods and pillars, drenching them in colour (see page 50). Climbing types are easier to prune than ramblers.

Arches and pergolas

↗ Ramblers, with their pliable stems, are ideal for training over arches and pergolas. However, unlike climbers, ramblers are not normally repeat-flowering (see page 51).

Tall tree stumps

↘ Old tree trunks, if still sturdy and not at risk from falling over under the weight of rose stems and foliage, can be clothed with foliage and flowers (see page 54).

Growing into trees

↓ Both climbing and rambling roses can be used, but they need to be vigorous. Once established, roses grown in this way need little attention (see page 54).

Seasonal displays

**Can I get
year-round
colour?**

By choosing a range of climbers and wall shrubs, it is possible to have walls, arches and trellises dressed in colour throughout the year. Some of these plants have radiant flower colours, others richly shaded and variegated leaves; there are many to choose from – see the **A–Z of climbers and wall shrubs** (pages 24–39) and **A–Z of climbing and rambling roses** (pages 40–47). Here is a cavalcade of climbers and wall shrubs for all seasons.

SEASONAL FAVOURITES

The range of these glorious plants is wide, but throughout the years several have come to epitomize perfection and therefore influence the choice of a climber or wall shrub. We all have our own cherished favourites, and a few are illustrated here for you to consider.

Before deciding on the climber of your choice, consider whether you want flowers, leaves, berries or seedheads. The choice is extensive and some have a dual role, such as *Clematis macropetala*, *Clematis montana* and *Clematis orientalis*, which have flowers as well as attractive seedheads.

Berried wall shrubs are other people's choices and few are as reliable as *Pyracantha* spp. and *Cotoneaster horizontalis*, which is ideal for clothing low walls. Some of these are sufficiently hardy to create magnificent displays in winter.

SPRING

SUMMER

↗ Clematis montana
Late spring and early summer
(see page 27)

↗ Wisteria floribunda
Late spring and early summer
(see page 31)

↗ Passiflora caerulea
Early to late summer
(see page 30)

↗ Solanum crispum
Early to late summer
(see page 30)

More spring favourites

- *Abeliophyllum distichum* (late winter to mid-spring) – see page 24.
- *Abutilon megapotamicum* (late spring to early autumn) – see page 24.
- *Ceanothus thyrsiflorus* var. *repens* (late spring and early summer) – see page 25.
- *Garrya elliptica* (catkins: late winter and early spring) – see page 29.
- *Wisteria sinensis* (late spring and early summer) – see page 31.

More summer favourites

- *Carpenteria californica* (early and mid-summer) – see page 25.
- *Clematis* – large-flowered hybrids (summer) – see page 27.
- *Clematis chrysocoma* (early and mid-summer) – see page 26.
- *Cytisus battandieri* (early summer) – see page 28.
- *Fremontodendron californicum* (throughout summer and into early autumn) – see page 28.
- *Lonicera japonica* (early summer to autumn) – see page 29.
- *Lonicera tragophylla* (early and mid-summer) – see page 30.
- *Trachelospermum jasminoides* (mid- and late summer) – see page 31.

FOLIAGE THROUGHOUT THE YEAR

Evergreen climbers with handsomely variegated leaves bring colour throughout the year, especially in late spring and early summer when new leaves start to appear. Many small- and large-leaved *Hedera* (Ivies) have variegated leaves and these can be grown up walls as well as on free-standing trellises (see pages 34–35 for details of these climbers).

Pyracantha spp. are hardy, evergreen shrubs, suitable for growing against walls, with foliage that is exceptionally attractive when it is covered with frost and snow. If there are berries present, this is a bonus (see page 39), as they are brightly coloured and show up well against white.

The variegated, small-leaved Hedera helix *'Goldheart' (Ivy) never fails to create an attractive display.*

ADDED SHELTER

Many popular garden shrubs that normally grow in borders benefit from the shelter of a wall, especially those that flower in late winter or spring. The well-known *Forsythia suspensa* (Golden Bell) that bears clusters of bright yellow for about a month in spring is one. *Kerria japonica* 'Pleniflora' (Bachelor's Buttons) is another – it creates a better display of double, yellow flowers during mid- and late spring when given shelter. For a large display, the slightly tender *Magnolia grandiflora* is also at its best grown against a wall. Its large, creamy-white flowers appear from mid- to late summer or early autumn.

AUTUMN **WINTER**

↗ Parthenocissus henryana
Autumn-coloured leaves
(see page 36)

↗ Vitis vinifera *'Purpurea'*
Autumn-coloured leaves
(see page 37)

↗ Cotoneaster horizontalis
Red berries
(see page 39)

↗ Pyracantha rogersiana *'Flava'*
Bright yellow berries
(see page 39)

More autumn favourites
• *Celastrus orbiculatus* (coloured leaves) – see page 36.
• *Clematis orientalis* (attractive seedheads) – see page 39.
• *Clematis vitalba* (attractive seedheads) – see page 39.
• *Parthenocissus quinquefolia* (coloured leaves) – see page 36.
• *Parthenocissus tricuspidata* (coloured leaves) – see page 37.
• *Vitis coignetiae* (coloured leaves) – see page 37.

More winter favourites
• *Chimonanthus praecox* (flowers: mid- and late winter)
  – see page 26.
• *Hedera canariensis* 'Gloire de Marengo' (attractive leaves)
  – see page 34.
• *Hedera colchica* 'Dentata Variegata' (attractive leaves)
  – see page 35.
• *Hedera colchica* 'Sulphur Heart' (attractive leaves)
  – see page 35.
• *Hedera helix* 'Goldheart' (attractive leaves)
  – see page 35.
• *Jasminum nudiflorum* (flowers: late autumn to late spring)
  – see page 29.

Autumn weather

Rich autumn leaf colours are encouraged by low temperatures and dry soil. Sudden temperature drops will trigger spectacular colours.

Buying a climber or wall shrub

How do I choose a good plant?

When buying a woody and perennial climber, it is usual to choose a container-grown plant. This is also the best option, because it ensures that there is little root disturbance when the plant is planted. Annual-type climbers raised as half-hardy plants (see pages 32–33) are usually bought established and growing in a pot. Always check the plant for pest and disease damage before buying, and that the compost is moist but not waterlogged.

CHOOSING AND BUYING

Container-grown plants

These are plants that are established and growing healthily in a container and are sold ready for planting into their growing positions. They are sold throughout the year and can be planted whenever the soil is workable and the weather not excessively cold. However, most of these plants are sold in spring and early summer.

What to look for

Check that the compost's surface is not covered in moss, nor that masses of roots are coming out of the drainage holes in the container's base. The plant must also be correctly labelled. Climbers should be well supported and secured (but not strangulated) and wall shrubs not congested or with branches interlaced. You should always view a plant from all sides before deciding whether or not to buy it.

Healthy leaves, stems and growing tips

Healthy flowers and buds, free from pests and diseases

Plants clearly labelled

No roots coming out of the container's base

Clean pot, free from dirt and algae

Inspect the plant, compost and pot before buying a climber. The presence of moss, algae or congested roots indicates neglect.

SHELTERING PLANTS

When slightly tender climbers or wall shrubs are being planted, cold winds may damage the foliage before they have a chance to become established. Temporarily protect plants by forming a screen on the windward side. This can be done by sandwiching straw between a piece of folded, plastic-coated wire-netting, which is then secured upright to two stout stakes.

When to buy

Although container-grown plants can be bought at any time of the year, spring and early summer are the best times as this gives the plant a long growing period to become established before the onset of cold weather in autumn. Do not buy a plant, either, until its planting and growing position has been prepared and a supporting framework has been set in place.

Best side forward

It is essential that the most attractive side on a wall shrub faces away from the wall and into the garden. However, it is possible to cut away an unsightly stem if the rest of the shrub's 'face side' is attractive. It may be also necessary to prune away branches that are growing strongly inwards and towards the wall.

Climbers do not usually have a face-side problem, but if the plant has a few flowers position them so that they face outwards and towards the front.

If a plant has to wait a few weeks before being planted, temporarily stand it in a wind-sheltered, well-drained position with the face side positioned outwards and towards the light.

WHERE TO BUY PLANTS

Always buy container-grown plants from a reputable source to guarantee a healthy, well-established root system. A poor and cheap climber or wall shrub seldom grows into a plant that creates a magnificent display for many years.

- **Garden centres** ~ these mainly sell container-grown plants, including climbers and wall shrubs. Check out the garden centre as well as its plants; if it looks neglected and radiates little pride, this may be reflected in the quality of the plants.

- **Nurseries** ~ these sell container-grown plants as well as bare-rooted types. Some nurseries specialize in specific plants, such as clematis, and this may mean a long journey or buying through a catalogue.

GETTING THE PLANT HOME

A car is usually essential. To ensure that your plant will arrive home safely, do not take children or dogs on the journey with you! Make a special visit to buy plants rather than squeezing them in between other shopping. Also remember to keep the plant away from draughts and strong sunlight while transporting it.

PLANTING A CLIMBER OR WALL SHRUB

Preparing the planting position

↗ Thorough soil preparation is essential to ensure rapid plant establishment and healthy growth.

During the months prior to planting, dig the soil and mix in plenty of decomposed garden compost or well-decayed manure. Remove perennial weeds, taking care not to leave even the smallest piece of root. About a week before planting (and after the support, such as trellis, has been put in place) thoroughly soak the soil with water, covering a wide area. Watering is essential, as soil near the base of a wall is invariably dry.

Preparing the plant

↗ Thoroughly water the compost the day before the climber or wall shrub is to be planted.

The day before planting a container-grown climber or wall shrub, stand the container on a well-drained surface and water the compost. If the compost is dry, water quickly runs out of the drainage holes; if this happens, water the compost again. If the plant has misplaced branches, use sharp secateurs to cut them out, close to their point of origin or just above a healthy bud.

Position the flowers so that they are facing outwards

Ensure that the plant is upright

Top of the soil ball must be slightly below the soil surface

Friable soil drawn around the soil ball and firmed

Planting a climber or wall shrub

Wait until the soil's surface is becoming dry before starting to plant. If planting is carried out when the soil is too wet, its structure will be damaged and planting is difficult.

- Dig out a hole, deep enough to accommodate the rootball and with its centre 30–45 cm (1–1½ ft) from the wall. Add further well-decomposed garden compost to the planting hole.
- Form and firm a slight mound in the hole's base, remove the container and place the soil ball in position. Check that the best side is outwards. The top of the soil ball should be slightly below the surface of the surrounding soil.
- Dribble friable soil around the soil ball and firm it in layers, not all at once. When the surface is reached, rake the surface level. Leaving depressions on the surface will cause puddles to form when the soil is watered.

↖ Careful and thorough planting is the first step in establishing a long-lived and attractive climber or wall shrub in your garden.

Watering

↗ Thoroughly water the soil without disturbing the surface. Use a rosed watering can.

When planting has been completed, check that the plant is labelled and, if it is a climber, there is a garden cane to guide its shoots to the base of a trellis or other support. Gently but thoroughly water the soil's surface to ensure that the underlying soil is moist but not waterlogged.

Mulching the soil

↗ Covering the soil around the plant with a mulch prevents the growth of weeds and conserves moisture in the soil.

After the soil has been watered, cover the surface for 45–60 cm (1½–2 ft) around the plant with a 5–7.5 cm (2–3 in) thick layer of well-decomposed garden compost. Keep the mulch away from the plant's stem. The mulch keeps the soil moist and cool, as well as preventing the growth of weeds.

Supporting a climber

Do all climbers need support?

Many climbers are self-supporting, while others clamber through a trellis or other supporting framework. The need for support also depends on where the climber is being grown. For example, climbers such as ivies are self-supporting and quickly scale walls, but when grown to separate one part of a garden from another, or to create a peep-proof screen, need a strong, free-standing trellis. Below are examples of the scaling habits of climbers.

CLIMBING HABITS

Each climber's growing habit indicates the type of support it needs to support its stems and flowers. The climbing styles of climbers can be arranged into four main groups.

Leaners

Jasminum nudiflorum

These climbers do not have any visible means of support and in the wild either lean against a support or grow through nearby plants. However, small leaning types grown in gardens need a supporting framework against which they can lean and be secured. Tall and vigorous ones are best left to scramble through trees and large shrubs. Examples of leaning climbers include:
• *Abutilon megapotamicum* (see page 24) • *Berberidopsis corallina* (see page 25) • *Jasminum nudiflorum* (see page 29) • Roses – climbing types (see pages 40–47) • *Solanum crispum* (see page 30)

Self-supporting climbers

Hedera colchica 'Dentata Variegata'

These climbers use aerial roots or adhesive suckers to scale walls and trees. However, where these plants are grown to form screens they need strong, free-standing trellises. Examples of these plants include: • *Hedera canariensis* 'Gloire de Marengo' (see page 34) • *Hedera colchica* 'Dentata Variegata' (see page 35) • *Hedera colchica* 'Sulphur Heart' (see page 35)
• *Hedera helix* 'Goldheart' (see page 35) – also known as *Hedera helix* 'Oro di Bogliasco' • *Hydrangea anomala* subsp. *petiolaris* (see page 29) • *Parthenocissus henryana* (see page 36) • *Parthenocissus quinquefolia* (see page 36) • *Parthenocissus tricuspidata* (see page 37) • *Parthenocissus tricuspidata* 'Veitchii' (see page 37)

Climbers with tendrils or twisting leaf-stalks

Passiflora caerulea

In the wild, these need twiggy hosts around which they can wrap tendrils or hook their leaf-stalks. In gardens, they are best supported by a trellis or other framework. Examples include: • *Clematis* – large-flowered hybrids (see pages 27–28) • *Clematis* 'Frances Rivis' (see page 26) • *Clematis armandii* (see page 26) • *Clematis chrysocoma* (see page 26) • *Clematis flammula* (see page 26)
• *Clematis macropetala* (see page 27) • *Clematis montana* (see page 27) • *Clematis orientalis* (see page 27) • *Clematis tangutica* (see page 28) • *Lathyrus odoratus* (page 33) • *Passiflora caerulea* (see page 30)

Twiners

Humulus lupulus 'Aureus'

In the wild, these climbers gain support by twining around neighbouring plants. In a garden, however, it is best to provide them with a supporting framework. Examples of these climbers include: • *Actinidia chinensis* (see page 34) – also known as *Actinidia deliciosa* • *Actinidia kolomikta* (see page 34) • *Akebia quinata* (see page 24) • *Humulus lupulus* 'Aureus' (see page 35) • *Jasminum officinale* (see page 29) • *Lonicera japonica* (see page 29) • *Lonicera periclymenum* 'Belgica' (see page 30) • *Lonicera periclymenum* 'Serotina' (see page 30) • *Lonicera tragophylla* (see page 30) • *Solanum laxum* (see page 30) – also known as *Solanum jasminoides* • *Wisteria floribunda* (see page 31) • *Wisteria sinensis* (see page 31)

SUPPORTING CLIMBERS WITH TRELLIS

Some climbers are self-supporting, clambering up walls or interlacing themselves with other plants, but the majority of climbers grown in gardens need a strong and durable trellis to which they can cling or be attached. The two main ways to support them is by attaching a trellis to a wall, or erecting a free-standing trellis which acts as a garden divider or screen. The construction of both these is illustrated and explained below. Some trellises have square holes; others are diamond-shaped and have a more informal appearance. Always select a trellis that suits the style of the garden – informal or formal.

ERECTING A TRELLIS AGAINST A WALL

Before securing a trellis to a wall, check that the brickwork is strong enough to take the weight of both the trellis and a mature plant. If the wall has been pebble-dashed (stoned) and painted, ensure that it is sound and, if possible, paint the area.

1 *Drill a hole in each corner to enable the trellis to be secured on a wall. Countersink each hole.*

2 *Position the trellis; use a spirit-level (carpenter's level) to ensure it is level. Mark the drilling positions on the wall.*

3 *With a masonry drill, drill holes about 6 cm (2½ in) deep. Insert a wall-fixing (anchor); the end should be flush with the wall.*

4 *Position the trellis; use galvanized screws to secure it. Place 2.5 cm (1 in) thick spacers between the wall and the trellis.*

ERECTING A FREE-STANDING TRELLIS

Free-standing trellises need sound construction, with posts well secured in concrete. The depth of the hole depends on the height of the screen (see below). In windy and exposed areas, and especially when the trellis is clad in evergreen climbers, increase the depths of the holes and lengths of the posts.

1 *Dig a hole to the required depth (see below), plus 15 cm (6 in). Put clean rubble in the base.*

2 *Put the post in the hole and check that it is upright. Use a builder's spirit-level (carpenter's level). Knock a stake into the soil at an angle of 45°, ready for securing the post temporarily.*

DEPTHS OF HOLES AND HEIGHTS OF POSTS

- **Post 1.2 m (4 ft) above ground:** needs a post 1.6 m (5½ ft) long, in a hole 45 cm (1½ ft) deep.

- **Post 1.5 m (5 ft) above ground:** needs a post 2.1 m (7 ft) long, in a hole 60 cm (2 ft) deep.

- **Post 1.8 m (6 ft) above ground:** needs a post 2.4 m (8 ft) long, in a hole 60 cm (2 ft) deep.

3 *Use a long nail to secure the stake to the post (two stakes may be needed). Check again that the post is vertical.*

4 *Use concrete to secure the post in position; then use a trowel to slope the concrete's surface away from the post.*

On a slope

When erecting a screen on a slope, keep the posts vertical, but with the panels level and staggered in height.

Pruning climbers and wall shrubs

Many climbers and wall shrubs benefit from yearly pruning. It prevents them becoming congested with dead, old and crossing stems. At the same time, it helps to extend their active and attractive life and, for flowering types, to produce a better display. Some of these plants need little pruning; others require detailed and regular attention. Below is an **A–Z** of pruning climbers and wall shrubs; pruning of climbing and rambling roses is covered on pages 18–19.

Is pruning necessary?

TOOLS YOU WILL NEED

Sharp secateurs that make clean cuts are essential. There are two types. **Bypass** secateurs (also known as parrot or cross-over secateurs) have a scissor-like action, and cut when one blade passes the other. The **anvil** type has a sharp blade that cuts when in contact with a firm, metal surface known as an anvil.

Secateurs
For general pruning

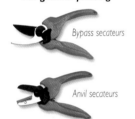

Bypass secateurs

Anvil secateurs

Long-handle secateurs
For out-of-easy-reach shoots

Bypass long-handle secateurs

Anvil long-handle secateurs

When to prune?

The time of year to prune a flowering climber or wall shrub is influenced by its flowering period relative to the onset of cold weather. The time to prune evergreen climbers, such as ivies, is not so critical and mainly involves reducing their size (sometimes twice a year).

KEY TO SYMBOLS *(used below)*

Each plant's nature is indicated by the following symbols:

 Climber   **Wall shrub**

A–Z OF PRUNING CLIMBERS AND WALL SHRUBS

Abeliophyllum distichum

 Little pruning is needed; cut out dead shoots in early spring or as soon as there is no risk of frost.

Abutilon megapotamicum

 In spring, cut out straggly and frost-damaged shoots.

Abutilon vitifolium

 Prune in the same way as for *Abutilon megapotamicum*.

Acacia

Wattle

 These slightly tender evergreen shrubs and trees are best grown against a warm, sheltered wall. Once established and with a framework of branches, little pruning is needed. Large specimens can be cut back radically after the flowers fade. This restricts their size – but do not do this too often, as each time a shrub is severely pruned it takes longer to recover. Never cut into really old wood.

Actinidia chinensis

Chinese Gooseberry / Kiwi Fruit; also known as *Actinidia deliciosa*

 No regular pruning is needed for ornamental specimens, but occasionally thin out and trim back long shoots in late winter.

Actinidia kolomikta

Kolomikta Vine

No regular pruning is needed... Prune as for *Actinidia chinensis*. Usually, it is left to cover a wall and only pruned when too large.

Akebia

 Little pruning is needed for this climbing, twining shrub, other than cutting out dead and long shoots in spring.

Ampelopsis

No regular pruning is needed, other than cutting out dead and overcrowded shoots in spring.

A–Z OF PRUNING CLIMBERS AND WALL SHRUBS (CONTINUED)

Aristolochia macrophylla

Dutchman's Pipe

 Little pruning is usually needed, but where space is limited thin out shoots and shorten long shoots by about one-third in late winter or early spring.

Azara

 No regular pruning is needed. However, where shoots are damaged by frost, or plants become 'leggy', cut stems back in late spring after the flowers fade.

Berberidopsis corallina

Coral Plant

 Little pruning is needed, other than cutting out dead shoots in late winter or early spring. Also cut out a few congested shoots so that light and air can enter.

Campsis radicans

Trumpet Vine

After planting, cut back all shoots to about 15 cm (6 in) high. This encourages the development of shoots from around the plant's base. With established plants, cut back the previous year's shoots to 5–7.5 cm (2–3 in) of their bases in late winter or early spring.

Carpenteria californica

 As soon as the flowers fade in mid- to late summer, shorten long, straggly and weak shoots.

Ceanothus cuneatus var. rigidus and Ceanothus thyrsiflorus var. repens

Californian Lilacs

No regular pruning is needed.

Celastrus orbiculatus

Oriental Bittersweet / Staff Vine

 When this plant is allowed to grow freely over a tree, no pruning is needed. However, when it is grown against a wall or over a pergola, thin out unwanted or misplaced shoots in early spring. Also cut back main shoots by half their length.

Chaenomeles

Cydonia / Japanese Quince

When grown as a wall shrub, cut back secondary shoots at the end of mid-spring or into late spring.

Chimonanthus praecox

Winter Sweet

 When this is planted against a wall, cut out all the flowered shoots to within a couple of buds of their base after the flowers fade.

CLEMATIS
Large-flowered hybrids (climbers)

These popular climbers were earlier given different pruning techniques according to their parentage, such as florida, patens, jackmanii, viticella and lanuginosa. However, as a result of hybridization during recent years these pruning divisions are now practically worthless. Therefore, it is far better to be guided by the times at which they flower.

Group 1 ~ Flowering initially from the latter part of late spring to mid-summer, they develop flowers mainly on short sideshoots on the previous season's growths. Sometimes, they develop further flowers at the tips of shoots produced during the same year. During a climber's early years, it is essential to encourage the development of shoots from the plant's base. Therefore, once established and during its second year, in spring cut all stems to within 23 cm (9 in) of the ground. During subsequent years, as soon as buds start to swell in spring, cut out weak and dead shoots. Tie shoots to the supporting framework.

Group 2 ~ Flowering from mid-summer onwards, they develop flowers from the leaf-joints of shoots produced earlier in the same year. Prune them in spring, removing dead shoots and cutting out those that flowered during the previous year to a pair of plump, healthy buds.

Clematis alpina

 Weak-growing deciduous climber with a bushy habit that needs little pruning other than cutting out faded flowers. It seldom becomes too large but, should this happen, cut back long shoots after the flowers fade, in late spring or early summer.

Clematis armandii

Vigorous evergreen climber that is best pruned as soon as the flowers fade, in late spring. Cut out all shoots that produced flowers.

Clematis chrysocoma

Deciduous climber, less vigorous than *Clematis montana* and better suited to small or medium-sized gardens. It flowers mainly during early and mid-summer, and sometimes later. Therefore, cut back long shoots as soon as the flowers fade. This produces shoots for flowering during the following year. Sometimes it flowers on shoots produced earlier during the current year. Where this climber is allowed to clamber into a tree, leave it unpruned.

A–Z OF PRUNING CLIMBERS AND WALL SHRUBS (CONTINUED)

Clematis flammula

Deciduous, bushy climber with flowers from late summer to mid-autumn. In late winter or early spring, cut back all shoots to strong buds at their base.

Clematis florida 'Sieboldiana'

Deciduous or semi-evergreen climber which flowers in late spring to early summer. Little pruning is needed; thin out congested plants after the flowers fade.

Clematis macropetala

Slender, deciduous climber which flowers in late spring and early summer. As soon as the flowers fade, cut back the shoots that produced them.

Clematis montana

Vigorous, deciduous climber that benefits from yearly pruning. After the flowers fade, in early summer, cut back all shoots that produced flowers. This encourages the development of young shoots that will flower during the following year. If clambering in a tree, leave it unpruned.

Clematis orientalis

Deciduous climber with flowers in late summer and into autumn. No regular pruning is needed, but thin out congested plants in spring.

Clematis rehderiana

Deciduous climber with flowers from late summer to autumn. No regular pruning is needed, but thin out congested plants in spring.

Clematis tangutica

Deciduous climber with flowers from late summer to mid-autumn. In late winter or early spring, cut back all shoots to strong buds at their base.

Cotoneaster horizontalis

Hardy, evergreen wall shrub. No regular pruning is needed.

Cytisus battandieri

Pineapple Broom

No regular pruning is needed.

Eccremocarpus scaber

Chilean Glory Flower

In late spring, cut out frost-damaged shoots. However, if the plant is severely damaged by frost, prune all stems to their bases in spring to encourage the development of fresh ones.

Fremontodendron californicum

No regular pruning is needed, other than cutting off frost-damaged shoots in spring.

Garrya elliptica

Silk-tassel Bush

When grown against a wall, cut back long, secondary shoots in spring, after the flowers fade.

Hedera

Ivies

In late spring or early spring, check that shoots are not becoming too invasive; cut them back, as necessary. Also, cut back long stems in late summer.

Humulus lupulus 'Aureus'

Yellow-leaved Hop

Herbaceous climber; in autumn or early winter the leaves die down. Remove these in either late autumn or spring.

Hydrangea anomala subsp. petiolaris

Japanese Climbing Hydrangea

No regular pruning is needed. However, cut out dead shoots in spring. Also, thin out congested and straggly shoots.

Jasminum nudiflorum

Winter-flowering Jasmine

In mid-spring, after the flowers fade, cut out to within 5–7.5 cm (2–3 in) of their bases all the stems that produced flowers. Also completely cut out weak and spindly shoots.

Jasminum officinale

Common White Jasmine

After the flowers fade, thin out flowered shoots to their base. Do not just shorten them.

Jasminum polyanthum

Pink Jasmine

In temperate climates, this climber is often grown indoors as a houseplant, but in warm areas it can be grown outdoors against a warm, wind-sheltered wall. No regular pruning is needed, other than occasionally thinning out overgrown plants after the flowers fade.

A–Z OF PRUNING CLIMBERS AND WALL SHRUBS (CONTINUED)

Lapageria rosea

Chilean Bell Flower

 Only half-hardy outdoors in temperate climates and therefore best grown against a warm wall. After the flowers fade in late summer or early autumn, thin out weak shoots. In cold areas leave this task until spring.

Lonicera japonica

Japanese Honeysuckle

 No regular pruning is needed, but occasionally thin out congested plants in late winter or early spring.

Lonicera periclymenum 'Belgica'

Early Dutch Honeysuckle

 No regular pruning is needed, other than occasionally thinning out old and congested shoots after the flowers fade.

Lonicera periclymenum 'Serotina'

Late Dutch Honeysuckle

 No regular pruning is needed, except occasionally cutting out old and congested shoots in spring.

Parthenocissus henryana

Chinese Virginia Creeper

 No regular pruning is needed. However, cut out congested and dead shoots in spring.

Parthenocissus quinquefolia

True Virginia Creeper

Prune in the same way as for *Parthenocissus henryana*, although it is much more vigorous and, therefore, more thinning is needed.

Parthenocissus tricuspidata

Boston Ivy

Prune in the same way as for *Parthenocissus quinquefolia*.

Passiflora caerulea

Common Passion Flower

In late winter or early spring, cut back old stems to ground level or to a main stem. Also cut back lateral shoots to 15 cm (6 in) long.

Pyracantha

Firethorn

 When grown against a wall, shorten long sideshoots in mid-spring. However, do not remove too many shoots as, if left, they produce flowers in the following year.

Schizophragma hydrangeoides

Japanese Hydrangea Vine

 In autumn, cut out dead flowers and unwanted shoots from wall-trained plants. Those which are clambering into trees can be left unpruned.

Schizophragma integrifolium

Prune in the same way as for *Schizophragma hydrangeoides*.

Solanum crispum

Chilean Potato Tree

 In mid-spring, trim back the previous season's growth to 15 cm (6 in) long. Also cut out weak shoots and those that have been killed by frost.

Solanum laxum

Jasmine Nightshade

 In spring, thin out weak shoots and cut out those that have been damaged by frost.

Trachelospermum asiaticum

 Where plants are becoming too large, in early or mid-spring thin out vigorous shoots.

Trachelospermum jasminoides

Star Jasmine

Prune in the same way as for *Trachelospermum asiaticum*.

Vitis

Regular pruning is not necessary, but where plants are congested thin out shoots in late summer.

Wisteria

Japanese and Chinese Wisteria

Wisterias need regular pruning to keep their growth in check and to encourage flowers. In late winter, cut back all shoots to within 2–3 buds of the point where they started to grow during the previous season. Where a plant is too large, also prune it in mid-summer; cut the current season's new shoots back to within 5–6 buds of their bases.

Pruning climbing roses

Is it easy to prune climbers?

How you prune a climbing rose is dictated by the type of climber you have. In general, climbers have a permanent or semi-permanent framework of shoots and it is from lateral shoots that flowers are borne. These shoots develop in spring and summer and bear flowers during the same year. There are several types of climber and they can be divided into two main groups, according to the way they are pruned. These varieties are listed below.

PRUNING NEWLY PLANTED CLIMBERS

Plant bare-rooted specimens during their dormant period, from late autumn to late winter. In spring, cut out dead wood, especially the tips of stems that have been damaged by frost. Secure the stems to a supporting framework, so that rain and wind cannot damage them. Ensure that the stems are firmly supported, but not strangled. Do not be tempted to cut down the stems after the climber has been planted; unlike for a rambling rose (which initially is radically pruned), the stems on climbers are left alone. During the autumn, use sharp secateurs to cut off the dead flowers.

PRUNING ESTABLISHED ROSES

Group 1 (see list below): Prune established roses in late winter or early spring. Little pruning is needed, other than the removal of dead wood and withered shoot tips. Lateral shoots which produced flowers during the previous year need to be cut back to about 7.5 cm (3 in) long.

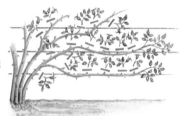

← *Pruning is relatively simple and this illustration shows how to prune varieties in Group 1.*

Group 2 (see list below): Prune established roses in late winter or early spring. Little pruning is needed – less than for those in Group 1. Cut out dead shoots, as well as withered shoot tips. Do not prune lateral shoots.

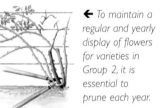

← *To maintain a regular and yearly display of flowers for varieties in Group 2, it is essential to prune each year.*

PRUNING GROUPS

Group 1
Varieties include:
- 'Casino' (pale yellow)
- 'Climbing Ena Harkness' (crimson-scarlet)
- 'Climbing Etoile de Hollande' (deep red)
- 'Madame Grégoire Staechelin' (pink, shaded crimson)
- 'Mermaid' (primrose-yellow)
- 'Parkdirektor Riggers' (blood-red)

Group 2
Varieties include:
- 'Aloha' (rose-pink)
- 'Altissimo' (red)
- 'Bantry Bay' (rose-pink)
- 'Breath of Life' (apricot)

- 'Climbing Cécile Brünner' (shell-pink)
- 'Climbing Crimson Glory' (crimson)
- 'Climbing Iceberg' (white)
- 'Climbing Lady Sylvia' (pale pink)
- 'Climbing Masquerade' (yellow, then pink and red)
- 'Climbing Mrs Sam McGredy' (coppery-orange)
- 'Climbing Super Star' (orange-vermilion)
- 'Compassion' (pink, shaded apricot)
- 'Danse du Feu' (orange-scarlet)
- 'Dortmund' (red, with a white eye)
- 'Galway Bay' (pink)

- 'Gloire de Dijon' (buff-yellow)
- 'Golden Showers' (golden-yellow)
- 'Guinée' (dark red)
- 'Handel' (cream, edged pink)
- 'Highfield' (pale yellow)
- 'Leverkusen' (pale yellow)
- 'Madame Alfred Carrière' (white, flushed pink)
- 'Maigold' (bronze-yellow)
- 'Meg' (pink, with apricot base)
- 'Morning Jewel' (pink)
- 'Pink Perpétué' (rose-pink)
- 'Rose Mantle' (deep rose-pink)
- 'Royal Gold' (deep yellow)

- 'Schoolgirl' (apricot-yellow)
- 'Swan Lake' (white, tinged pink)
- 'White Cockade' (white)
- 'Zéphirine Drouhin' (carmine-pink)

Climbers that cannot be identified

You may have a climber that is not on this list. If it flowers mainly on lateral shoots, treat it as a plant in Group 1.

Pruning rambling roses

The stems on newly planted ramblers need radical pruning. This is because, unlike climbers, they develop long, flexible stems and do not have a permanent framework. Their flowers are borne on shoots which developed during the previous year. This indicates the basic pruning technique; as soon as they finish flowering, these shoots are cut out. For detailed pruning purposes, ramblers are divided into three groups (see below for relevant varieties).

Do ramblers need severe pruning?

PLANTING AND PRUNING RAMBLING ROSES

Plant bare-rooted ramblers from late autumn to late winter. Sometimes the stems have been shortened by the nursery before despatch. However, before planting them, cut all shoots back to 23–38 cm (9–15 in) long. Also cut back damaged and coarse roots. Plant the rambler slightly deeper than before, and firm friable soil over and around the roots. During spring, young shoots will grow from the tops of the shoots and later create a colourful array of flowers.

Pruning a pillar rose

Pillar roses are useful for creating height and focal points in a garden – and are relatively inexpensive to create. They form beacons of interest and are easy to create and prune. Erect a support, about 2.4 m (8 ft) high, formed of a rustic pole with its branches cut to leave 15–20 cm (6–8 in) stubs. These stubs give support to the rose's stems and help to prevent them falling sideways.

Plant bare-rooted pillar roses from late autumn to late winter. Tie the long stems to the pole. During summer, lateral shoots will develop on the stems. Cut off the flowers as soon as they have faded. In early winter, cut back the laterals that produced flowers, at the same time removing all weak, diseased and thin shoots.

During the following summer (and in all subsequent years), the lateral shoots on the old wood will bear flowers. Cut these off when they fade, and in early winter cut back the laterals that produced the flowers.

PRUNING ESTABLISHED RAMBLING ROSES

Group 1 (see list below): Prune established ramblers in autumn, cutting down to ground level all stems that produced flowers during that season. Tie in the new stems that developed during the same year – and will produce flowers during the following year – to their supports. If the rambler has not produced many new stems, retain some of the older ones and trim their lateral stems to about 7.5 cm (3 in) long. Sometimes it is difficult to sort out the canes, because they may have developed into a near thicket. If this happens, just cut back lateral shoots to 7.5 cm (3 in) from the main stems.

PRUNING GROUPS

Group 1
Varieties include:
- 'American Pillar' (deep pink, with white eye)
- 'Crimson Shower' (crimson)
- 'Dorothy Perkins' (rose-pink)
- 'Excelsa' (rosy-crimson, with white centre)
- 'François Juranville' (pale pink)
- 'Sander's White Rambler' (white)
- 'Seagull' (white)

Group 2
Varieties include:
- 'Albéric Barbier' (cream)
- 'Albertine' (pale pink)
- 'Paul's Scarlet Climber' (scarlet)
- 'Veilchenblau' (violet, shading to slate-grey)

Group 3
Varieties include:
- 'Emily Gray' (buff-yellow)
- Rosa filipes 'Kiftsgate' (creamy-white)
- 'Wedding Day' (creamy-white)

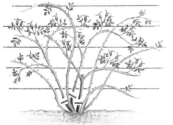

← *This illustration shows how to prune varieties in Group 1.*

Group 2 (see list left): Prune established ramblers in autumn, cutting all shoots that produced flowers back to a point where new and vigorous shoots have developed. Also cut back 1–2 old stems to 30–38 cm (12–15 in) above the soil. As with Group 1, sometimes it is difficult to sort out the canes. In this case, just cut back lateral shoots to 7.5 cm (3 in) from the main stems.

Group 3 (see list left): Pruning established ramblers in this group is easy. In autumn, prune them lightly, cutting out old and dead wood and the tips of lateral shoots that have flowered.

Increasing climbers

Are they easy to propagate?

Climbers and wall shrubs can be increased in several different ways. Some are simple and easy, such as sowing hardy annual climbers outdoors or dividing herbaceous types. Other methods take longer to establish new plants, and these include sowing seeds in greenhouses and taking cuttings. These propagation methods demand a range of techniques, but none of them is beyond the capabilities of home gardeners and only a few need specialist equipment.

SOWING SEEDS

Hardy annual climbers

Seeds of hardy annual climbers are sown directly into the positions in which the plants will grow and, later, produce flowers. These plants have a single-season life-span.

1 *Use a straight-edged stick for guidance and a thin, pointed one to form shallow drills.*

2 *Tip a few seeds into the palm of your hand and sow them thinly and evenly in the drill.*

3 *Use the back of a metal rake to draw soil over the seeds. Firm with the head of the rake.*

Applies to these plants

- *Ipomoea purpurea* (Common Morning Glory) – see page 32. Can also be raised in gentle warmth in a greenhouse.

- *Lathyrus odoratus* (Sweet Pea) – see page 33. Can also be raised in gentle warmth in a greenhouse.

- *Lophospermum scandens* 'Jewel Mixed' – see page 33.

- *Maurandella antirrhiniflora* 'Mixed' – see page 33.

- *Tropaeolum majus* (Garden Nasturtium) – see page 33.

- *Tropaeolum peregrinum* (Canary Creeper) – see page 33. Can also be raised in gentle warmth in a greenhouse.

Sowing seeds in seed-trays (flats) in greenhouses

Some annual climbers are raised in gentle warmth in a greenhouse in late winter or early spring, and planted outdoors when the weather is free from frost.

1 *Gently firm compost in a seed-tray (flat). Tip seeds into a V-shaped piece of paper; tap it to spread them over the compost.*

2 *Lightly cover the seeds with compost by using a flat-based horticultural sieve. Alternatively, use an old culinary type of sieve.*

3 *Stand the seed-tray (flat) in clean water until moisture seeps to the surface. Remove and let excess water drain away.*

LATER ...

4 *After germination, reduce the temperature and give the seedlings more light. Before they become congested, transfer them to wider spacings in seed-trays (flats) (see 5), but do not damage the roots. The day before transferring seedlings, gently water the compost.*

5 *To move the seedlings into further seed-trays (flats), use a small dibber (dibble); space out the seedlings, but do not put them close to the edge. Gently firm the compost, then water from above.*

Applies to these plants

- *Caiophora lateritia* 'Frothy' – see page 32.

- *Cobaea scandens* (Cathedral Bells) – see page 32.

- *Lathyrus odoratus* (Sweet Pea) – see page 33. Can also be sown outdoors.

- *Lophospermum scandens* 'Jewel Mixed' – see page 33.

- *Maurandella antirrhiniflora* 'Mixed' – see page 33.

- *Thunbergia alata* (Black-eyed Susan) – see page 33.

- *Tropaeolum peregrinum* (Canary Creeper) – see page 33. Can also be sown outdoors.

Please note: some annual plants can be raised as hardy annuals as well as half-hardy annuals.

DIVISION

Dividing clumps of herbaceous climbers is an easy and assured way to increase them. Always select healthy plants.

➔ In autumn or late winter, cut down all stems to ground level. Use a garden fork to dig up the clump, and then two forks positioned back to back in the centre of the clump to lever it apart. Divide small pieces by hand. Replant young pieces from around the outside of the clump.

Applies to this plant

• The popular *Humulus lupulus* 'Aureus' (Golden-leaved Hop; featured on page 35) is easily increased by division. Indeed, it is better to divide it every 3–4 years than leave it to create an exceptionally large clump.

TAKE CARE ...

Do not allow the roots to become dry before replanting. If the weather is hot, cover them with wet sacking.

HALF-RIPE CUTTINGS

Also known as semi-hardwood and semi-mature cuttings, half-ripe cuttings are formed of shoots that are more mature than softwood types but not as old and tough as hardwood types.

1 *Take half-ripe cuttings during mid-summer. Remove 7.5–10 cm (3–4 in) long shoots, preferably with pieces of older wood (known as heels) attached to their bases.*

2 *Remove the lower leaves and trim the cutting's base, cutting off whisker-like growths. These heels encourage rapid rooting.*

3 *Insert each cutting in a pot of equal parts moist peat and sharp sand. Firm the compost and water from above.*

Applies to these plants

Many climbers and wall shrubs can be raised from half-ripe cuttings and these are indicated in the A–Z of Climbers and Wall Shrubs (see pages 24–47). These range from *Abeliophyllum distichum*, with its honey-scented, late winter flowers, to the leafy *Parthenocissus* species, which include the Virginia Creeper and other climbers that produce glorious autumn-coloured leaves.

HARDWOOD CUTTINGS

These are formed of mature shoots from the current season's growth and are taken mainly from early to late autumn. They are tougher and harder than half-ripe cuttings.

➔ Hardwood cuttings are variable in length from 15 to 38 cm (6–15 in) but are usually 23–30 cm (9–12 in). Most are taken from deciduous plants and therefore by the time cuttings are prepared they are bare of

leaves. Cut the base below a bud, and the top to just above a healthy, mature bud. Insert cuttings in V-shaped trench, with one vertical side and half to two-thirds the length of the cutting deep – usually 15–20 cm (6–8 in). Sprinkle sharp sand in the base and stand spaced-out cuttings on top. Return friable soil to the trench and firm it with your foot. Rooting takes up to a year.

Routine care of climbers and wall shrubs

What do I need to do?

Like all plants, climbers and wall shrubs need regular attention. Many need yearly pruning (see pages 14–19), while others create colourful flowers or leaves each year without any intervention, especially when growing into tall trees. There are also routine tasks, some that encourage the rapid establishment of plants. Supporting structures, such as trellises, pergolas and arches, need a yearly check to ensure they will not collapse when laden with flowers and leaves.

KNOW YOUR PLANTS

The choice of climbing plants is wide, ranging from annuals and herbaceous perennials to woody and perennial types. Wall shrubs are woody and 'permanent'. They all need slightly different treatment.
- Annual climbers, after creating a magnificent display during the summer, are then pulled up and discarded. Similarly, herbaceous types die down to soil level in autumn, and their leaves and stems need to be removed by the following early spring.
- Woody and perennial climbers will be with you for many years, and once established many need little attention, apart from pruning.
- Wall shrubs will last for many years, perhaps 15 or more. Many need to be pruned each year (see pages 14–17).

GETTING PLANTS ESTABLISHED

All plants need careful attention during the first few weeks or months after being planted. This is the period when their roots are becoming established and, if the soil becomes dry, growth is retarded. Perpetually dry soil may even cause a plant's death.

Most 'getting established' tasks are routine gardening jobs, and in spring include refirming soil loosened by severe winter frost and removing weeds which, if left, would be in competition with the climber or wall shrub for moisture and food. Also, if left they may suffocate small climbers. A yearly mulch also helps to keep the soil cool and moist, as well as free from weeds.

Firming soil in spring

↗ In spring, refirm the soil around plants to ensure it is in close contact with the roots. Use the heel of your shoe or boot; when complete, rake the surface level.

Removing weeds

↗ Use a hand fork to dig out the roots of perennial weeds, taking care not to leave a broken part in the soil. Put annual weeds on a compost heap, but burn perennial types.

Watering the soil

→ Keep the soil moist, especially if the climber or wall shrub is newly planted. Soil around the base of a wall is usually dry and therefore regular watering is essential.

Forming a yearly mulch

→ In spring of each year, shallowly mix the previous year's mulch into the soil and apply a further 5–7.5 cm (2–3 in) thick layer of well-decomposed garden compost.

CHECKING SUPPORTS

Wooden posts and trellises, as well as rustic poles used for informal arches and pergolas, have a limited life-span and need to be regularly checked, especially in exposed areas and in preparation for winter winds. Autumn is the best time to check and replace posts. If the base of a planed, square-section post has decayed, the whole post needs to be replaced or a metal post spike fitted to its base.

Checking trellises Unless a trellis is drenched in the leaves of an evergreen climber, parts of it are usually visible and the onset of decay is easily spotted. If only a few pieces of internal timbers have rotted away, they can be replaced by fresh ones nailed into place. Usually, however, the problem is far more radical and rather than patching up a trellis a replacement will be needed. This is best undertaken in autumn or winter; in order to prevent the climber being damaged, carefully cut away the trellis, replace it and tie stems into place.

Checking wall-fixings (anchors) However strong the original wall-fixings may be, after ten or more years they will inevitably become loosened by wind pressure on the trellis, as well as by the effects of rain. Galvanized screws have a long life, but even they will eventually succumb to rust. Part of the problem is that brickwork eventually falls away. The easiest remedy for this is to take down the trellis, remove the wall-fixings (anchors), redrill the wall and use larger ones. If this poses a problem, redrill the trellis and wall. By carefully moving the trellis, it is sometimes possible to push the wall-fixing (anchor) into place, realign the trellis and use a new screw.

RENOVATING A NEGLECTED CLIMBER

Many deciduous climbers if neglected become a mass of old, tangled, woody stems. The climber's base becomes bare and unsightly, with a poor display of flowers. Most climbers can be renovated by severe pruning, especially if in good general health. Climbers that are weak and with little new growth each year should first be fed and thoroughly watered for a season.

Renovation pruning is best spread over 2–3 years. At the same time, feed and regularly water the plant.

During the first year – and before cutting out a proportion of old stems – cut out dead and diseased shoots back to healthy buds. Then, cut out to near ground level a proportion of the old stems. Most neglected climbers can withstand having their stems cut close to ground level in spring. Use secateurs or long-handled loppers to cut down old stems. If there are some new stems, leave these in place. In one of the two following years, cut down the other old stems.

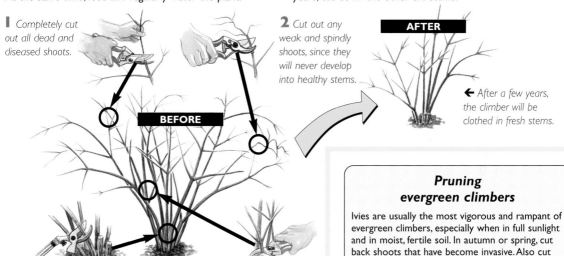

1 *Completely cut out all dead and diseased shoots.*

2 *Cut out any weak and spindly shoots, since they will never develop into healthy stems.*

BEFORE

AFTER

← *After a few years, the climber will be clothed in fresh stems.*

3 *Over 2–3 years, each spring cut out to near ground level a proportion of the old stems.*

4 *If there are young stems, leave these in place, but remove congested, twiggy shoots.*

Pruning evergreen climbers

Ivies are usually the most vigorous and rampant of evergreen climbers, especially when in full sunlight and in moist, fertile soil. In autumn or spring, cut back shoots that have become invasive. Also cut out old shoots.

Be prepared for plants to be dirty and dusty; if necessary, wear protective goggles and a gauze breathing mask.

RENOVATING CLIMBERS AND WALL SHRUBS

- Honeysuckles, such as *Lonicera japonica*, *Lonicera periclymenum* 'Belgica' and *Lonicera periclymenum* 'Serotina', eventually become a tangled mass of old stems if pruning is neglected. If this happens, in spring cut the complete plant to 38–50 cm (15–20 in) of the ground.

- *Pyracantha* spp. grown against walls can be rejuvenated by cutting back all stems to old wood in spring. However, this will mean sacrificing flowers for a few seasons.
- Many clematis that have become a tangled mass of stems can be cut to ground level in spring.

Flowers

Are all flowering climbers hardy?

Climbers and wall shrubs vary in their ability to survive outdoors in temperate climates, but the majority of the plants featured throughout this book are fully hardy and reliable. Those that need special attention and planting are indicated. However, even in temperate climates temperatures are influenced by the latitude, altitude and aspect of your locality – but there will always be a climber or wall shrub to suit your garden and your personal taste.

Arches clothed in flowering climbers are ideal for separating parts of a garden.

INFORMAL OR FORMAL?

Some climbers have an informal and relaxed nature, while others are better suited for formal gardens, and it is essential to select ones that will complement their surroundings. For example, *Lonicera* spp. (Honeysuckles) have a casual appearance, many with the bonus of lingering and rich fragrances. In contrast, wisterias have a more formal habit, especially when clothing a formal pergola made out of planed wood. Indeed, often it is the structure of a pergola or trellis that initially dictates the choice of the right style of climber.

The art of using climbing plants in formal garden displays is discussed on pages 70–71, while attractive associations of climbers and wall shrubs are detailed on pages 62–67.

SCENTED GARDENS

Fragrant flowers add an exciting quality to gardens and there are many climbers, wall shrubs and roses to choose from. Many of these plants are described – together with their fragrances – on pages 58–61.

Abeliophyllum distichum
Slightly tender deciduous shrub with star-shaped, white, honey-scented flowers borne on bare stems during late winter and mid-spring.
Soil and situation: moderately fertile, well-drained but moisture-retentive soil. A position against a sheltered, sunny wall is essential.
Raising new plants: take 7.5–10 cm (3–4 in) long cuttings from half-ripened shoots in mid-summer and insert in pots; place in gentle warmth. Also layer low-growing stems.
Cultivation: provide support.

⬆ 1.2–1.8 m (4–6 ft) ↔ 1.5–1.8 m (5–6 ft)

Abutilon megapotamicum
Tender, slender-stemmed, evergreen shrub with narrowly pointed and coarsely toothed leaves. From late spring to early autumn it bears pendent, scarlet and yellow flowers.
Soil and situation: well-drained but moisture-retentive soil and a wind-sheltered position against a sunny wall.
Raising new plants: take 7.5–10 cm (3–4 in) long cuttings from half-ripe shoots during mid- and late summer; insert them in pots and place in gentle warmth.
Cultivation: provide support.

⬆ 1.2–1.5 m (4–5 ft) ↔ 1.2–1.8 m (4–6 ft)

Akebia quinata
Chocolate Vine UK/USA
Five-finger Akebia USA
Vigorous, twining climber, usually deciduous but evergreen in mild areas, with leaves formed of five pear-shaped leaflets. During late spring it produces vanilla-scented, reddish-purple flowers. Sometimes, these are followed by sausage-shaped fruits.
Soil and situation: well-drained soil.
Raising new plants: the easiest way is to layer low-growing stems.
Cultivation: it is best when grown up a pillar, rather than against a wall.

⬆ 4.5–6 m (15–20 ft) or more ↔ 1.2–m (4 ft) or more

Aristolochia macrophylla
Dutchman's Pipe UK/USA

Hardy, vigorous, deciduous climber with large, broadly heart-shaped green leaves and pipe-like, yellow, brown and green flowers up to 36 mm (1½ in) long during early summer.

Soil and situation: fertile, well-drained soil in sun or partial shade.

Raising new plants: layer low-growing shoots in autumn, sow seeds in spring or take cuttings in mid-summer and place in gentle warmth.

Cultivation: provide support.

↥ 3.6–4.5 m (12–15 ft) or more ↔ 1.8 m (6 ft) or more

Azara microphylla

Tender, evergreen shrub or small tree. Dainty, dark green leaves appear in large sprays; in early spring it bears clusters of vanilla-scented yellow flowers.

Soil and situation: well-drained, moisture-retentive soil and a sunny, sheltered wall.

Raising new plants: take 7.5 cm (3 in) long cuttings from half-ripened shoots in spring and insert in pots; place in gentle warmth.

Cultivation: provide support.

↥ 3–3.6 m (10–12 ft) ↔ 1.5–1.8 m (5–6 ft)

Berberidopsis corallina
Coral Plant UK/USA

Slightly sparse, evergreen shrub with spine-edged leaves and clusters of pendent, rounded, deep red flowers during mid- and late summer, and sometimes later.

Soil and situation: moisture-retentive but well-drained, slightly acid, cool soil.

Raising new plants: either layer low-growing shoots or take cuttings in mid-summer.

Cultivation: shaded position against a sheltered wall.

↥ 1.2–1.8 m (4–6 ft) ↔ 1.5–2.1 m (5–7 ft)

Carpenteria californica
Tree Anemone UK/USA

Slightly tender evergreen shrub with bright green leaves and fragrant white flowers, up to 7.5 cm (3 in) wide, during early and mid-summer.

Soil and situation: well-drained, light, neutral or slightly chalky soil, in full sun and against a wind-sheltered wall.

Raising new plants: during spring, sow seeds in loam-based seed compost and place in gentle warmth. Later, transfer seedlings to individual pots and place in a cold frame.

Cultivation: a support is essential.

↥ 2.4–3 m (8–10 ft) ↔ 1.8–2.4 m (6–8 ft)

Ceanothus cuneatus var. rigidus
Californian Lilac UK

Also known as *Ceanothus rigidus*, this slightly tender evergreen shrub bears purple-blue flowers in mid-spring.

Soil and situation: moderately fertile, well-drained but moisture-retentive, neutral or slightly acid soil. Plant in a sunny position.

Raising new plants: during mid-summer, take 7.5–10 cm (3–4 in) long heel cuttings and insert in equal parts moist peat and sharp sand in pots.

Cultivation: provide support.

↥ 1.8–3 m (6–10 ft) ↔ 1.2–1.5 m (4–5 ft)

Ceanothus thyrsiflorus var. repens
Californian Lilac UK

Hardy, evergreen shrub with small leaves and clusters of light blue flowers during late spring and early summer.

Soil and situation: moderately fertile, well-drained but moisture-retentive, neutral or slightly acid soil in full sun.

Raising new plants: during mid-summer, take 7.5–10 cm (3–4 in) long heel cuttings; insert in equal parts moist peat and sharp sand in pots in a propagation frame.

Cultivation: a support may be needed.

↥ 1.2–1.5 m (4–5 ft) ↔ 1.5–1.8 m (5–6 ft)

Chimonanthus praecox

Also known as *Chimonanthus fragrans*, this deciduous shrub has spicy-scented, cup-shaped flowers with yellow petals and purple centres from mid- to late winter. 'Grandiflorus' has larger flowers, with red centres.

Soil and situation: well-drained but moisture-retentive soil and a warm position against a wind-sheltered wall.

Raising new plants: layer low-growing shoots in late summer.

Cultivation: no support is needed.

↕ 1.8–3 m (6–10 ft) ↔ 2.4–3 m (8–10 ft)

Clematis armandii

Hardy evergreen climber with masses of saucer-shaped, creamy-white flowers during mid- and late spring. 'Apple Blossom' has pink and white flowers.

Soil and situation: fertile, neutral to slightly alkaline, moisture-retentive but well-drained soil in full sun. Ensure the roots are shaded.

Raising new plants: during mid-summer, take 7.5–10 cm (3–4 in) long cuttings and insert in equal parts moist peat and sharp sand in pots. Place them in gentle warmth.

Cultivation: provide support.

↕ 7.5–9 m (25–30 ft) ↔ 7.5–9 m (25–30 ft)

Clematis chrysocoma

Hardy, deciduous climber with single, saucer-shaped white flowers, about 5 cm (2 in) wide, with a pink tinge, in early and mid-summer – and sometimes later.

Soil and situation: fertile, neutral to slightly alkaline, moisture-retentive but well-drained soil in full sun. Shade roots.

Raising new plants: during mid-summer, take 7.5–10 cm (3–4 in) long cuttings and insert in equal parts moist peat and sharp sand in pots. Place them in gentle warmth.

Cultivation: provide support.

↕ 3–3.6 m (10–12 ft) ↔ 3–4.5 m (10–15 ft)

Clematis flammula

Fragrant Virgin's Bower UK

Hardy, deciduous, scrambling climber with hawthorn-scented, white flowers from late summer to mid-autumn.

Soil and situation: fertile, neutral to slightly alkaline, moisture-retentive but well-drained soil in full sun. Shade roots.

Raising new plants: during mid-summer, take 7.5–10 cm (3–4 in) long cuttings and insert them in equal parts moist peat and sharp sand in pots; place in gentle warmth.

Cultivation: provide support.

↕ 3 m (10 ft) ↔ 1.8–2.4 m (6–8 ft)

Clematis florida 'Sieboldiana'

Usually deciduous (sometimes semi-evergreen) shrubby climber with leaves formed of nine leaflets and with double, saucer-shaped, white flowers with purple centres mainly during early summer.

Soil and situation: fertile, neutral to slightly alkaline, moisture-retentive but well-drained soil in full sun. Shade roots.

Raising new plants: during mid-summer, take 7.5–10 cm (3–4 in) long cuttings. Place them in gentle warmth.

Cultivation: provide support.

↕ 2.4–3 m (8–10 ft) ↔ 1–1.2 m (3½–4 ft)

Clematis 'Frances Rivis'

Earlier known as *Clematis alpina* 'Frances Rivis', this free-flowering deciduous climber has pendulous, violet-blue flowers during mid- and late spring.

Soil and situation: fertile, neutral to slightly alkaline, moisture-retentive but well-drained soil in full sun. Shade roots.

Raising new plants: take 7.5–10 cm (3–4 in) long half-ripe cuttings during mid-summer. Insert them in pots in slight warmth.

Cultivation: provide support.

↕ 1.8–2.4 m (6–8 ft) ↔ 1.2–1.8 m (4–6 ft)

Clematis macropetala

Hardy, moderately vigorous, deciduous and bushy climber with light and dark blue, nodding, bell-shaped flowers during late spring and early summer.

Soil and situation: fertile, neutral to slightly alkaline, moisture-retentive but well-drained soil in full sun. Shade roots.

Raising new plants: during mid-summer, take 7.5–10 cm (3–4 in) long cuttings and insert in equal parts moist peat and sharp sand in pots. Place them in gentle warmth.

Cultivation: provide support.

↕ 3–3.6 m (10–12 ft) ↔ 1.8–2.4 m (6–8 ft)

Clematis 'Marie Boisselot'
Large-flowered hybrid

Hardy, deciduous climber with large, pure white flowers with creamy stamens from early to late summer.

Soil and situation: fertile, neutral to slightly alkaline, moisture-retentive but well-drained soil in full sun. Shade roots.

Raising new plants: during mid-summer, take 7.5–10 cm (3–4 in) long cuttings and insert them in equal parts moist peat and sharp sand in pots. Place them in gentle warmth.

Cultivation: provide support.

↕ 3–4.5 m (10–15 ft) ↔ 1.2–1.8 m (4–6 ft)

Clematis montana
Mountain Clematis UK

Hardy, vigorous, deciduous climber with masses of pure white, slightly scented flowers in late spring and early summer.

Soil and situation: fertile, neutral to slightly alkaline, moisture-retentive but well-drained soil in full sun. Shade roots.

Raising new plants: during mid-summer, take 7.5–10 cm (3–4 in) long cuttings and insert them in equal parts moist peat and sharp sand in pots; place in gentle warmth.

Cultivation: provide support.

↕ 5.4–7.5 m (18–25 ft) ↔ 5.4–7.5 m (18–25 ft)

Clematis 'Mrs Cholmondeley'
Large-flowered hybrid

Hardy, deciduous, free-flowering climber with large, pale blue flowers from early to late summer.

Soil and situation: fertile, neutral to slightly alkaline, moisture-retentive soil in full sun. Shade roots.

Raising new plants: during mid-summer, take 7.5–10 cm (3–4 in) long cuttings and insert them in equal parts moist peat and sharp sand in pots. Place them in gentle warmth.

Cultivation: provide support.

↕ 3–4.5 m (10–15 ft) ↔ 1.2–1.8 m (4–6 ft)

Clematis 'Nelly Moser'
Large-flowered hybrid

Hardy, deciduous climber with large flowers, blush white with a central carmine bar, during early summer and, again, in late summer and early autumn.

Soil and situation: fertile, neutral to slightly alkaline, moisture-retentive soil in full sun. Shade roots.

Raising new plants: during mid-summer, take 7.5–10 cm (3–4 in) long cuttings and insert them in equal parts moist peat and sharp sand in pots. Place them in gentle warmth.

Cultivation: provide support.

↕ 3–4.5 m (10–15 ft) ↔ 1.2–1.8 m (4–6 ft)

Clematis orientalis
Orange-peel Clematis UK

Hardy, vigorous, deciduous climber with fern like leaves. Nodding, yellow, star-like, fragrant flowers appear from late summer to mid-autumn.

Soil and situation: fertile, neutral to slightly alkaline, moisture-retentive but well-drained soil in full sun. Shade roots.

Raising new plants: during mid-summer, take 7.5–10 cm (3–4 in) long cuttings and insert them in equal parts moist peat and sharp sand in pots. Place them in gentle warmth.

Cultivation: provide support.

↕ 3–6 m (10–20 ft) ↔ 3–6 m (10–20 ft)

Clematis rehderiana

Hardy, deciduous, vigorous climber with nodding, cowslip-scented, soft primrose-yellow flowers during late summer and into early autumn.

Soil and situation: fertile, neutral to slightly alkaline, moisture-retentive but well-drained soil in full sun. Shade roots.

Raising new plants: during mid-summer, take 7.5–10 cm (3–4 in) long cuttings and insert them in equal parts moist peat and sharp sand in pots. Place them in gentle warmth.

Cultivation: provide support.

⬆ 4.5–6 m (15–20 ft) or more ⬌ 1.5–1.8 m (5–6 ft) or more

Clematis tangutica

Hardy, deciduous, vigorous, fast-growing climber with grey-green leaves and lantern-shaped, rich yellow flowers from late summer to mid-autumn.

Soil and situation: fertile, neutral to slightly alkaline, moisture-retentive but well-drained soil in full sun. Shade roots.

Raising new plants: during mid-summer, take 7.5–10 cm (3–4 in) long cuttings and insert them in equal parts moist peat and sharp sand in pots. Place them in gentle warmth.

Cultivation: provide support.

⬆ 4.5–6 m (15–20 ft) ⬌ 2.1–3 m (7–10 ft)

Clematis 'Ville de Lyon'
Large-flowered hybrid

Hardy, deciduous climber with large, bright carmine-red flowers, shading to crimson around the edges, from mid-summer to early autumn.

Soil and situation: fertile, neutral to slightly alkaline, moisture-retentive but well-drained soil in full sun. Shade roots.

Raising new plants: during mid-summer, take 7.5–10 cm (3–4 in) long cuttings and insert them in equal parts moist peat and sharp sand in pots. Place them in gentle warmth.

Cultivation: provide support.

⬆ 3–4.5 m (10–15 ft) ⬌ 1.2–1.8 m (4–6 ft)

Cytisus battandieri
Moroccan Broom UK

Pineapple Broom UK

Large, slightly tender deciduous shrub with golden-yellow, pineapple-scented flowers during early summer.

Soil and situation: poor to fairly rich, neutral, light, well-drained soil in a position against a sunny wall.

Raising new plants: raise from seeds sown in spring and place in a cold frame.

Cultivation: plant against a warm wall.

⬆ 3–4.5 m (10–15 ft) ⬌ 2.4–3.6 m (8–12 ft)

Fallopia baldschuanica
Mile-a-minute Vine UK

Russian Vine UK

Hardy, deciduous, vigorous climber with pale pink or white flowers borne in fleece-like clusters up to 45 cm (18 in) long from mid-summer to autumn.

Soil and situation: poor to moderately fertile, well-drained but moisture-retentive soil and any aspect.

Raising new plants: during mid- and late summer take 7.5–10 cm (3–4 in) long cuttings; insert in pots and place in a cold frame.

Cultivation: provide support.

⬆ 9–12 m (30–40 ft) ⬌ 9–12 m (30–40 ft)

Fremontodendron californicum

Slightly tender, deciduous or semi-evergreen shrub with cup-shaped, golden-yellow, 5 cm (2 in) wide flowers from late spring to autumn. 'Californian Glory' is a free-flowering form.

Soil and situation: moderately fertile, light, well-drained but moisture-retentive soil and a sheltered position in full sun.

Raising new plants: during early and mid-spring, sow seeds evenly and thinly 3 mm (⅛ in) deep in seed-trays (flats) in gentle warmth.

Cultivation: support is essential.

⬆ 1.8–3 m (6–10 ft) ⬌ 1.8–2.4 m (6–8 ft)

Garrya elliptica
Silk Tassel UK/USA

Hardy, evergreen shrub with thick, leathery leaves and drooping, grey-green catkins up to 23 cm (9 in) long during late winter and early spring.

Soil and situation: well-drained soil in full sun or light shade. However, flowering is best when in good light.

Raising new plants: take 7.5–10 cm (3–4 in) long cuttings from half-ripe sideshoots in late summer. Insert them in pots and place in a cold frame.

Cultivation: no support is needed.

↕ 2.1–3 m (7–10 ft) or more ↔ 1.8–2.1m (6–7 ft) or more

Hydrangea anomala subsp. petiolaris
Japanese Climbing Hydrangea UK

Also known as *Hydrangea petiolaris*, this hardy, vigorous, deciduous climber has creamy-white flowers borne in flat heads to 25 cm (10 in) wide in early summer.

Soil and situation: fertile, moisture-retentive but well-drained soil.

Raising new plants: during mid-summer, take 7.5 cm (3 in) long cuttings and insert in pots of equal parts moist peat and sharp sand in pots. Place them in a cold frame.

Cultivation: provide support.

↕ 9 m (30 ft) ↔ 9 m (30 ft)

Jasminum nudiflorum
Winter-flowering Jasmine UK

Hardy, deciduous, lax, wall shrub with pliable stems that bear bright yellow flowers, each up to 2.5 cm (1 in) wide, from late autumn to late spring. They are borne on bare stems.

Soil and situation: ordinary, well-drained soil against a shady wall.

Raising new plants: the easiest way to increase it is to layer low-growing stems in early or mid-autumn. They take about a year to produce roots.

Cultivation: provide support.

↕ 1.2–1.8 m (4–6 ft) ↔ 1.5–1.8 m (5–6 ft)

Jasminum officinale
Common White Jasmine UK

Poet's Jessamine UK/USA

Hardy, vigorous, deciduous climber with a twining habit. From early summer to autumn it bears clusters of pure white flowers.

Soil and situation: well-drained but moisture-retentive soil and a warm, sheltered position preferably in full sun.

Raising new plants: during autumn, layer low-growing stems. Alternatively, in late summer take half-ripe heel cuttings and insert in pots in gentle warmth.

Cultivation: provide support.

↕ 6–7.5 m (20–25 ft) ↔ 5.4–6 m (18–20 ft)

Lapageria rosea
Chilean Bell Flower UK/USA

Half-hardy, evergreen climber that for success outdoors needs a warm, sheltered position. Alternatively, it can be grown in a greenhouse. Pendent, bell-shaped, rose-crimson flowers from mid-summer to autumn.

Soil and situation: well-drained but moisture-retentive, neutral or slightly acid soil.

Raising new plants: layer low shoots in spring. Alternatively, sow seeds in gentle warmth in spring.

Cultivation: provide support.

↕ 2.1–3.6 m (7–12 ft) ↔ 1.5–2.1 m (5–7 ft)

Lonicera japonica
Japanese Honeysuckle UK/USA

Hardy, slow-growing, evergreen climber with fragrant, white to pale yellow, flowers from early summer to autumn.

Soil and situation: moderately fertile, well-drained but moisture-retentive soil, in full sun or, preferably, partial shade.

Raising new plants: during mid- and late summer take 7.5 cm (3 in) long cuttings; insert in pots in a cold frame. Also, layer low-growing shoots in autumn.

Cultivation: provide support.

↕ 4.5–7.5 m (15–25 ft) ↔ 3–4.5 m (10–15 ft)

Lonicera periclymenum 'Belgica'

Early Dutch Honeysuckle UK/USA

Hardy, deciduous climber with sweetly scented, purplish-red and yellow, flowers during late spring and early summer.

Soil and situation: moderately fertile, well-drained but moisture-retentive soil in full sun or, preferably, partial shade.

Raising new plants: during mid- and late summer take 10 cm (4 in) long cuttings; insert in a cold frame. Also, layer low-growing shoots in autumn.

Cultivation: provide support.

⬆ 4.5–6 m (15–20 ft) ↔ 3.6–4.5 m (12–15 ft)

Lonicera periclymenum 'Serotina'

Late Dutch Honeysuckle UK/USA

Hardy, deciduous climber with sweetly scented flowers, reddish-purple on the outside and creamy-white inside, from mid-summer to autumn.

Soil and situation: moderately fertile, well-drained but moisture-retentive soil in full sun or, preferably, partial shade.

Raising new plants: during mid- and late summer take 10 cm (4 in) long cuttings; insert in pots in a cold frame. Also, layer low-growing shoots during autumn.

Cultivation: provide support.

⬆ 4.5–6 m (15–20 ft) ↔ 3.6–4.5 m (12–15 ft)

Lonicera tragophylla

Chinese Woodbine UK

Hardy, vigorous, deciduous climber with whorls of golden-yellow flowers during early and mid-summer.

Soil and situation: moderately fertile, well-drained but moisture-retentive soil in full sun or, preferably, partial shade. Ensure the roots are shaded.

Raising new plants: during mid- and late summer take 10 cm (4 in) long cuttings; insert in a cold frame. Also, layer low-growing shoots in autumn.

Cultivation: provide support.

⬆ 3.6–5.4 m (12–18 ft) ↔ 3–4.5 m (10–15 ft)

Passiflora caerulea

Blue Passion Flower USA

Common Passion Flower UK

Slightly tender, more or less evergreen climber with 7.5 cm (3 in) wide flowers from early to late summer. Each has white petals and blue-purple stamens.

Soil and situation: poor to moderately fertile, well-drained but moisture-retentive soil and a warm, sheltered position.

Raising new plants: in mid-summer take 7.5–10 cm (3–4 in) long cuttings and insert in pots in gentle warmth.

Cultivation: provide support.

⬆ 1.8–4.5 m (6–15 ft) ↔ 1.8–4.5 m (6–15 ft)

Solanum crispum

Chilean Potato Tree UK

Slightly tender, bushy and scrambling, semi-evergreen climber with purple-blue, star-shaped flowers with prominent anthers from early to late summer. 'Glasnevin' is slightly hardier and more floriferous.

Soil and situation: moderately fertile, well-drained but moisture-retentive soil, in full sun or partial shade.

Raising new plants: during mid-summer, take 7.5 cm (3 in) long cuttings and insert in pots in gentle warmth.

Cultivation: provide support.

⬆ 3–6 m (10–20 ft) ↔ 3–6 m (10–20 ft)

Solanum laxum

Jasmine Nightshade UK

Potato Vine USA

Moderately hardy, evergreen shrub, also known as *Solanum jasminoides*, with twining stems and clusters of star-shaped, pale blue, flowers with golden anthers from mid-summer to autumn.

Soil and situation: moderately fertile, well-drained but moisture-retentive soil, in full sun or partial shade.

Raising new plants: during mid-summer, take 7.5 cm (3 in) long cuttings and insert in pots in gentle warmth.

Cultivation: support is essential.

⬆ 3–4.5 m (10–15 ft) ↔ 2.4–3.6 m (8–12 ft)

Trachelospermum jasminoides

Star Jasmine UK/USA

Hardy, evergreen climber with small, fragrant, white flowers in lax clusters during mid- and late summer.

Soil and situation: light, poor to moderately fertile, well-drained but moisture-retentive, slightly acid soil and a warm position.

Raising new plants: during mid- and late summer take 7.5–10 cm (3–4 in) long cuttings; insert in pots in gentle warmth. Alternatively, layer low-growing shoots in late summer or early autumn.

Cultivation: provide support.

↕ 3–4.5 m (10–15 ft)　↔ 3–4.5 m (10–15 ft)

Wisteria floribunda

Japanese Wisteria UK/USA

Hardy, vigorous, deciduous climber with fragrant, violet-blue flowers in spectacular, pendent clusters up to 30 cm (12 in) long during late spring and early summer. there is also a white-flowered form.

Soil and situation: fertile, moisture-retentive but well-drained soil and a sheltered position in full sun.

Raising new plants: in mid-summer, take 7.5–10 cm (3–4 in) long cuttings and insert in pots in gentle warmth.

Cultivation: provide support.

↕ 7.5–9 m (25–30 ft) or more　↔ 7.5–9 m (25–30 ft) or more

Wisteria sinensis

Chinese Wisteria UK/USA

Hardy, exceptionally vigorous, deciduous climber with fragrant, mauve flowers in pendent clusters up to 30 cm (12 in) long during late spring and early summer. 'Alba' has white flowers.

Soil and situation: Fertile, moisture-retentive but well-drained soil and a sheltered position in full sun.

Raising new plants: in mid-summer, take 7.5–10 cm (3–4 in) long cuttings and insert in pots in gentle warmth.

Cultivation: provide support.

↕ 15 m (50 ft) or more　↔ 15 m (50 ft) or more

MORE FLOWERING CLIMBERS

In addition to the climbers illustrated and described in this A–Z of flowering climbers, there are many others that create spectacular displays. These include:

• *Akebia trifoliata* (Three-leaved Akebia): also known as *Akebia lobata*, this vigorous, twining, deciduous climber, which is evergreen in mild areas, bears chocolate-coloured flowers during late spring. These are followed by violet-coloured, sausage-shaped fruits that are about 13 cm (5 in) long. It is ideal for growing against walls, as well as on rustic pergolas.

• *Clematis heracleifolia*: a distinctive clematis with a herbaceous nature and usually growing 90 cm–1.2 m (3–4 ft) high in a border. However, it can be given supports for it to clamber over and to create height variations in a border. Tubular, purple-blue flowers appear in clusters during late summer and into early autumn.

• *Jasminum humile* 'Revolutum' (Italian Yellow Jasmine): a straggly, evergreen shrub often grown against a wall. It needs a warm, wind-sheltered position; throughout summer it produces terminal clusters of small, fragrant, yellow flowers.

• *Jasminum* x *stephanense*: a deciduous or semi-evergreen climber with a twining and clambering habit, ideal for pergolas and arches. In early summer it produces 5–7.5 cm (2–3 in) long clusters of fragrant, pale pink flowers.

• *Lonicera* x *americana* (Honeysuckle): a vigorous, deciduous climber that soon covers trellises with large clusters of fragrant, yellowish, with a purple suffusion, flowers during the latter part of early summer and into mid-summer. Each flower is about 5 cm (2 in) long and 3.5 cm (1½ in) across.

• *Lonicera caprifolium* (Italian Woodbine/Perfoliate Woodbine/Goat-leaf Woodbine): a vigorous, deciduous climber with an informal habit and fragrant, creamy-white flowers tinged pink during the latter part of early summer and into mid-summer. It is ideal for clothing rustic pergolas or trellises in cottage gardens.

• *Lonicera sempervirens* (Trumpet Honeysuckle/Coral Honeysuckle): a vigorous climbing shrub, slightly tender in cold, temperate areas. In warm areas, it remains evergreen but is usually partially deciduous. In cold areas, it is ideal for growing in a large conservatory. From early to late summer, it produces slender clusters of flowers, rich orange scarlet on the outside and orange-yellow inside.

• *Lonicera* x *tellmanniana*: a beautiful hybrid honeysuckle with a strong-growing habit but slightly tender nature; for this reason, it is best grown against a warm, wind-sheltered wall. During early and mid-summer, it bears whorls of red and yellow flowers.

• *Schizophragma integrifolium*: a hardy, deciduous climber, ideal for clothing a trellis against a wall or pergola. It can also be used to clothe a tree trunk. From mid-summer to early autumn it produces small, white flowers ringed by long, white bracts.

Climbing annuals

Seeds of annual climbers are sown each year, either in seed-trays (flats) in gentle warmth or directly into their growing and flowering positions. The method depends on the nature of the plant, and this is detailed for each of the annuals described on these pages. You should always buy fresh seeds from a reputable seed company, as this gives a better chance of success than saving your own, and order your seeds early to ensure they arrive before their sowing dates.

BIT OF A CAPER!

The South American annual *Tropaeolum majus* (Nasturtium) was in earlier times cultivated for its flower buds and unripe seeds which, when pickled, were used as a substitute for capers to flavour vinegar and food.

OTHER ANNUAL CLIMBERS

In addition to the selection of plants illustrated on these pages, there are two other annual climbers that are well worth considering for inclusion as vertical interest in your garden.

- *Eccremocarpus scaber* (**Chilean Glory Flower/Glory Flower**): an evergreen climber, only half-hardy in most temperate regions and therefore usually grown as an annual. From early summer to autumn it bears orange-scarlet flowers.
- *Ipomoea tricolor* '**Heavenly Blue**' (**Morning Glory**): also known as *Ipomoea rubro-caerulea*, *Pharbitis tricolor* and *Ipomoea violacea*, this half-hardy perennial is usually grown as an annual. Sky-blue flowers are produced from mid- to late summer.

Tropaeolum majus (Nasturtium) plants have a relaxed and informal appearance and are ideal for clambering over rustic fencing.

Caiophora lateritia 'Frothy'
Biennial or short-lived perennial, usually grown as a half-hardy annual. From early to late summer it bears 5 cm (2 in) wide flowers that change from coppery-orange to white.

Soil and situation: fertile, moisture-retentive but well-drained soil in full sun.

Raising new plants: sow seeds in seed-trays (flats) in gentle warmth in spring and plant outside in small groups when all risk of frost has passed.

Cultivation: it delights in climbing through small shrubs.

↕ 1.2–1.8 m (4–6 ft) ↔ 60–90 cm (2–3 ft)

Cobaea scandens
Cathedral Bells UK
Half-hardy perennial usually grown as a half-hardy annual with bell-shaped, velvety-purple flowers and with a green base. It flowers throughout summer.

Soil and situation: moderately fertile, well-drained soil in full sun and with shelter from cold wind. Avoid rich soil.

Raising new plants: sow seeds in gentle warmth in mid-spring and plant the young plants outdoors when the risk of frost has passed.

Cultivation: support is essential.

↕ 3–3.6 m (10–12 ft) ↔ 1.5–2.1 m (5–7 ft)

Ipomoea purpurea
Common Morning Glory UK/USA
Also known as *Convolvulus major* and *Pharbitis purpurea*, this hardy annual displays large, funnel-shaped, 7.5 cm (3 in) wide purple flowers from mid-summer to the frosts of autumn.

Soil and situation: fertile, light, well-drained but moisture-retentive soil in full sun and sheltered from strong wind.

Raising new plants: sow seeds during late spring where plants are to grow and flower.

Cultivation: provide support.

↕ 2.4–3 m (8–10 ft) ↔ 1.5–2.1 m (5–7 ft)

Lathyrus odoratus

Sweet Pea UK/USA

Hardy annual with masses of fragrant flowers from early to late summer. Wide colour range, including shades of red, blue, pink and purple, as well as white.

Soil and situation: fertile, moisture-retentive soil in full sun.

Raising new plants: during late winter and early spring, sow seeds in gentle warmth. Acclimatize plants to outdoor temperatures and plant into a garden during late spring or early summer, depending on the climate.

Cultivation: provide support.

↕ 1.8–3 m (6–10 ft) ↔ 1.5–2.1 m (5–7 ft)

Lophospermum scandens 'Jewel Mixed'

Climbing Snapdragon UK/USA

Usually sold as *Asarina scandens* 'Jewel Mixed', this half-hardy perennial is usually grown as a half-hardy annual. Violet, white, pink and deep blue flowers from mid-summer to autumn.

Soil and situation: fertile, well-drained but moisture-retentive soil in full sun.

Raising new plants: during spring, sow seeds thinly and evenly in seed-trays (flats) and place in gentle warmth. Alternatively, sow seeds in late spring or early summer where plants are to grow.

Cultivation: supports are essential.

↕ 1.2–2.4 m (4–8 ft) ↔ 30–60 cm (1–2 ft) or more

Maurandella antirrhiniflora 'Mixed'

Twining Snapdragon UK/USA

Usually sold as *Asarina antirrhiniflora* 'Mixed', this tender perennial climber is usually grown as a half-hardy annual. From spring to autumn it bears purple or white, Snapdragon-like flowers.

Soil and situation: fertile, well-drained but moisture-retentive soil in full sun.

Raising new plants: during spring, sow seeds in seed-trays (flats) in gentle warmth. Alternatively, sow seeds in late spring or early summer where the plants are to grow.

Cultivation: provide support.

↕ 1.2–1.8 m (4–6 ft) ↔ 60–90 cm (2–3 ft)

Thunbergia alata

Black-eyed Susan UK

Half-hardy annual climber with distinctive white, yellow or orange flowers, each with a characteristic chocolate-brown eye, from early summer to early autumn.

Soil and situation: moderately fertile, well-drained but moisture-retentive soil in a sunny, wind-sheltered position.

Raising new plants: sow seeds 6 mm (¼ in) deep in pots in early or mid-spring; place in gentle warmth. Plant in a garden when risk of frost has passed.

Cultivation: provide support.

↕ 1.8–3 m (6–10 ft) ↔ 1.5–1.8 m (5–6 ft)

Tropaeolum majus

Garden Nasturtium USA

Indian Cress UK/USA

Nasturtium UK/USA

Hardy annual with a climbing or trailing habit, faintly scented from early summer to early autumn. There are varieties in red, pink, maroon, yellow and orange.

Soil and situation: poor, well-drained but moisture-retentive soil in full sun. Avoid excessively fertile soils.

Raising new plants: during mid- and late spring, sow seeds 6–12 mm (¼–½ in) deep where they are to flower.

Cultivation: provide support.

↕ 1.8–2.4 m (6–8 ft) ↔ 90 cm–1.4 m (3–4 ft)

Tropaeolum peregrinum

Canary Creeper UK/USA

Canary-bird Flower USA

Half-hardy, short-lived perennial usually grown as a hardy annual, with blue-green, five-lobed leaves and irregularly shaped, canary-yellow flowers, each with a green spur, from mid-summer to the frosts of autumn.

Soil and situation: fertile, well-drained but moisture-retentive soil in full sun.

Raising new plants: during mid- and late spring, sow seeds 6–12 mm (¼–½ in) deep where plants are to grow.

Cultivation: provide support.

↕ 1.8–3 m (6–10 ft) ↔ 1.2–1.4 m (2–4 ft)

Attractive leaves

Are these interesting all year?

Most of the climbers with attractive leaves described on these pages are evergreen and create eye-catching features throughout the year. However, the leaves are usually fresher and more vibrant in spring and early summer. Other climbers are deciduous or herbaceous, losing their canopy of foliage in autumn and creating a fresh, radiant display during the following spring and early summer. Remember to choose a climber with vigour to suit its allotted space.

LEAVES FOR ALL PLACES

The range of leaf colour and shape in climbing plants is wide, and includes dominantly variegated types such as *Hedera helix* 'Goldheart', with shiny green leaves splashed with yellow, and *Jasminum officinale* 'Aureum', which has leaves that are attractively blotched and suffused in a light yellow. When you are choosing a climber for your garden, remember to check that it will not dominate any nearby plants or pieces of statuary.

Just because a climber has small leaves, as in the case of *Hedera helix* 'Goldheart', do not assume that it will be 'demure' in nature; a wall that is totally covered with small, strongly coloured leaves usually has a greater colour impact when viewed from a distance than a large-leaved type that only sparsely covers a wall.

Variegated ivies are ideal for creating attractive backdrops for statues throughout the year.

IVY FOLKLORE

Ivy has been claimed to bring good luck to women, and to help girls find a husband.

Greek priests gave wreaths of ivy to newly married couples as emblems of fidelity.

Actinidia chinensis
Chinese Gooseberry UK/USA

Also known as *Actinidia deliciosa*, this vigorous, slightly tender, deciduous climber has large, heart-shaped, dark green leaves. Creamy-white flowers from early to late summer.

Soil and situation: fertile, well-drained, moisture-retentive, preferably slightly acid soil. Full sun or part shade.

Raising new plants: in mid-summer, take 7.5–10 cm (3–4 in) long cuttings and insert in equal parts moist peat and sharp sand in pots in gentle warmth.

Cultivation: supports are essential.

↕ 6–7.5 m (20–25 ft) or more ↔ 6–7.5 m (20–25 ft) or more

Actinidia kolomikta
Kolomikta Vine UK

Hardy, deciduous, spreading wall shrub with dark green leaves with white or pink areas at their tips and upper parts.

Soil and situation: fertile, well-drained, moisture-retentive, preferably slightly acid soil. Full sun or part shade.

Raising new plants: in mid-summer, take 7.5–10 cm (3–4 in) long cuttings and insert them in equal parts moist peat and sharp sand in pots; place in gentle warmth.

Cultivation: provide support.

↕ 2.4–3.6 m (8–12 ft) ↔ 2.4–4.5 m (8–15 ft)

Hedera canariensis 'Gloire de Marengo'

Also known as *Hedera canariensis* 'Variegata', this hardy, vigorous, evergreen climber has large, thick and leathery, deep green leaves with edges merging into silvery-grey and white.

Soil and situation: moderately fertile, well-drained but moisture-retentive soil in full sun or partial shade.

Raising new plants: during mid-summer, take 7.5–13 cm (3–5 in) long cuttings and insert them in equal parts moist peat and sharp sand in pots; place in gentle warmth.

Cultivation: it is self-clinging.

↕ 4.5–6 m (15–20 ft) ↔ 4.5–6 m (15–20 ft)

Hedera colchica 'Dentata Variegata'

Also known as *Hedera colchica* 'Dentata Aurea', this hardy, vigorous, evergreen climber has thick, leathery, bright green leaves, up to 20 cm (8 in) long, with pale green and creamy-white edges.

Soil and situation: moderately fertile, well-drained but moisture-retentive soil in full sun or partial shade.

Raising new plants: during mid-summer, take 7.5–13 cm (3–5 in) long cuttings and insert them in equal parts moist peat and sharp sand in pots; place in gentle warmth.

Cultivation: it is self-clinging.

↕ 6–7.5 m (20–25 ft) ↔ 6–7.5 m (20–25 ft)

Hedera colchica 'Sulphur Heart'

Also known as *Hedera colchica* 'Paddy's Pride', this hardy, vigorous, evergreen climber has thick, broadly oval, leathery, deep green leaves splashed and irregularly streaked bright yellow.

Soil and situation: moderately fertile, well-drained but moisture-retentive soil in full sun or partial shade.

Raising new plants: during mid-summer, take 7.5–13 cm (3–5 in) long cuttings and insert them in equal parts moist peat and sharp sand in pots; place in gentle warmth.

Cultivation: it is self-clinging.

↕ 5.4–6 m (18–20 ft) ↔ 5.4–6 m (18–20 ft)

Hedera helix 'Goldheart'

Also known as *Hedera helix* 'Oro di Bogliasco', this hardy, vigorous, evergreen climber has small, shiny-green leaves with yellow splashes at their centres.

Soil and situation: poor to moderately fertile, well-drained but moisture-retentive soil in full sun or partial shade.

Raising new plants: during mid-summer, take 7.5 cm (3 in) long cuttings from the current season's growth and insert them in equal parts moist peat and sharp sand in pots in gentle warmth.

Cultivation: it is self-clinging.

↕ 3.6–7.5 m (12–25 ft) ↔ 3.6–7.5 m (12–25 ft)

Humulus lupulus 'Aureus'

Golden-leaved Hop UK

Hardy, vigorous, herbaceous climber with scrambling stems densely clothed in 3–5-lobed, yellowish-green leaves.

Soil and situation: fertile, moisture-retentive but well-drained soil in full sun. High fertility is essential.

Raising new plants: in autumn or spring, use a garden fork to dig up the roots and divide them. Replant young pieces from the edges of the clump.

Cultivation: in autumn, cut away and dispose of old stems.

↕ 1.8–3 m (6–10 ft) ↔ 1.8–3 m (6–10 ft)

Jasminum officinale 'Aureum'

Also known as *Jasminum officinale* 'Aureovariegatum', this slightly tender deciduous climber has leaves blotched and suffused yellow.

Soil and situation: moderately fertile, well-drained but moisture-retentive soil and a sheltered position in full sun.

Raising new plants: during late summer, take 7.5–10 cm (3–4 in) long heel cuttings and insert in equal parts moist peat and sharp sand in pots. Place them in slight warmth.

Cultivation: provide support.

↕ 4.5–6 m (15–20 ft) ↔ 3–4.5 m (10–15 ft)

Lonicera japonica 'Aureoreticulata'

Also known as *Lonicera japonica* 'Variegata', this slightly tender, evergreen or semi-evergreen, climber has oblong to oval, light green leaves with their midribs and veins attractively lined in yellow. In exceptionally cold winters, stems and leaves die back to soil-level. Unfortunately, it seldom flowers.

Soil and situation: fairly fertile, well-drained soil in full sun or light shade.

Raising new plants: layer low-growing shoots in late summer or early autumn.

Cultivation: provide support.

↕ 1.2–2.4 m (4–8 ft) ↔ 1.2–1.5 m (4–5 ft)

Autumn-coloured foliage

Most autumn-coloured climbers are vigorous and ideal for clothing large walls. Some, such as *Parthenocissus* spp., can also be used to clamber into trees, while *Vitis vinifera* 'Purpurea' (Teinturier Grape) looks superb on a pergola on an informal patio or straddling a path. It is also known as the Dyer's Grape because earlier it was used to add colour to wine. *Parthenocissus henryana* (Chinese Virginia Creeper) is more slow-growing, especially when young.

Where can I grow them?

Climbers that become richly covered in autumn-coloured leaves are superb for creating dominant features on pergolas.

DOMINANT CLIMBERS

Many autumn-coloured climbers have an exceptionally vigorous nature, and rapidly clothe pergolas and large walls with rich colours. Therefore, you should always choose them with care; it will be easier to restrict a vigorous climber when it is clothing a pergola than when it is clambering up a wall. In addition, there is then less chance of it trespassing on a neighbour's property and causing friction.

CLIMBER OR VINE?

In Europe, climbing plants are known as 'climbers', but in North America they are referred to as 'vines', whatever their habit or species.

Because climbers are often grown close to a wall, where the soil is usually drier than in the open garden, they seldom fail to create superb colour features in autumn; in borders, however, autumn-coloured shrubs - especially if the soil is wet – are often less willing to produce their stunning colours, even though the temperature may be low.

Celastrus orbiculatus

Bittersweet UK/USA

Oriental Bittersweet USA

Hardy, deciduous, vigorous climber with mid-green leaves that in autumn assume clear yellow shades.

Soil and situation: poor to moderately fertile, moisture-retentive but well-drained soil and a sheltered position in full sun. Avoid chalky soils.

Raising new plants: sow seeds in early winter. Layer young shoots in autumn.

Cultivation: provide support. It will also clamber into trees.

↕ 6–9 m (20–30 ft) ↔ 6–7.5 m (20–25 ft)

Parthenocissus henryana

Chinese Virginia Creeper UK

Hardy, deciduous climber with dark green leaves variegated white and pink. In autumn, the variegation intensifies and the green becomes a brilliant red.

Soil and situation: moderately fertile, well-drained but moisture-retentive soil in full sun and in the shelter of a wall.

Raising new plants: in late summer, take 10 cm (4 in) long cuttings from the current season's growth and insert in pots in gentle warmth.

Cultivation: it is self-clinging, but nevertheless benefits from support.

↕ 6–7.5 m (20–25 ft) ↔ 3.6–4.5 m (12–15 ft)

Parthenocissus quinquefolia

True Virginia Creeper UK

Virginia Creeper UK/USA

Hardy, vigorous, deciduous climber with five-lobed (occasionally three) leaves that in autumn assume rich scarlet and orange shades.

Soil and situation: fertile, moisture-retentive soil in full sun or partial shade.

Raising new plants: during late summer, take 10 cm (4 in) long cuttings from the current season's growth and insert in pots in gentle warmth.

Cultivation: it is self-clinging.

↕ 10.5–18 m (35–60 ft) or more ↔ 10.5 m (35 ft) or more

Parthenocissus tricuspidata

Boston Ivy UK/USA

Japanese Creeper UK/USA

Also known as *Vitis inconstans*, this hardy, vigorous, deciduous climber has leaves that in autumn assume rich scarlet and crimson shades.

Soil and situation: fertile, moisture-retentive soil in full sun or partial shade.

Raising new plants: during late summer, take 10 cm (4 in) long cuttings from the current season's growth and insert in pots. Place in gentle warmth.

Cultivation: it is self-clinging.

↥ 9–12 m (30–40 ft) ↔ 6–9 m (20–30 ft)

Parthenocissus tricuspidata 'Veitchii'

Hardy, vigorous, deciduous climber with leaves tinged purple when young. In autumn the leaves assume rich scarlet and crimson shades.

Soil and situation: fertile, moisture-retentive soil in full sun or partial shade.

Raising new plants: during late summer, take 10 cm (4 in) long cuttings from the current season's growth and insert in pots in gentle warmth.

Cultivation: it is self-clinging.

↥ 9–12 m (30–40 ft) ↔ 6–9 m (20–30 ft)

Vitis amurensis

Amurland Grape UK

Hardy, deciduous, vigorous climber with large, dark green leaves – usually five-lobed, mid-green and downy below – that in autumn turn rosy-red, crimson and purple.

Soil and situation: moderately fertile, well-drained but moisture-retentive, slightly chalky soil. It grows well in most aspects.

Raising new plants: during early winter take 25–30 cm (10–12 in) long hardwood cuttings and insert in a sheltered position outdoors.

Cultivation: provide support.

↥ 7.5–12 m (25–40 ft) or more ↔ 7.5–6 m (25–30 ft) or more

Vitis coignetiae

Crimson Glory Vine UK/USA

Japanese Crimson Glory Vine UK

Hardy, vigorous, deciduous climber with large, rounded but lobed, mid-green leaves. In autumn, they assume rich colours – first yellow, then orange-red and, later, crimson.

Soil and situation: moderately fertile, well-drained, moisture-retentive, slightly chalky soil. It thrives in most aspects.

Raising new plants: layer low-growing shoots in autumn.

Cultivation: it is self-clinging.

↥ 12 m (40 ft) or more ↔ 12 m (40 ft) or more

Vitis vinifera 'Purpurea'

Dyer's Grape UK

Teinturier Grape UK

Hardy, deciduous climber with large, rounded and lobed, claret-red leaves that in autumn deepen to rich purple. Also, dark, purple fruits.

Soil and situation: moderately fertile, well-drained, moisture-retentive, slightly chalky soil. It thrives in most aspects.

Raising new plants: during early winter take 25–30 cm (10–12 in) long hardwood cuttings and insert in a sheltered position outdoors.

Cultivation: provide support.

↥ 4.5–5.4 m (15–18 ft) ↔ 4.5–5.4 m (15–18 ft)

OTHER AUTUMN-COLOURED CLIMBERS

- *Parthenocissus himalayana* var. *rubrifolia* (**Himalayan Virginia Creeper**): also known as *Parthenocissus himalayana* 'Purpurea', this vigorous, hardy, deciduous climber has leaves formed of three leaflets which assume brilliant scarlet colours in autumn. Additionally, in spring it has young, purplish leaves before becoming green.

- *Parthenocissus thomsonii*: a hardy, deciduous climber with leaves formed of five leaflets, wine-red in spring and becoming purple-crimson in autumn. This climber is not as vigorous as most related species and is ideal for clothing a pergola or wall.

- *Vitis davidii*: a hardy, deciduous climber with large, heart-shaped leaves, bronze-green when young and changing to rich crimson in autumn. It is not as vigorous as most *Vitis* species, but is ideal for clambering into a tree and clothing a pergola. Additionally, it develops small, black, edible grapes.

Seedheads, fruits and berries

How can I brighten winter?

The range of seedheads, fruits and berries is wide and certain to create attractive features during winter. Fluffy seedheads and berries are especially attractive when covered with frost, while red berries on *Cotoneaster horizontalis* (Fishbone Cotoneaster) become strongly contrasted by snow. Some berries on wall shrubs are yellow and are especially eye-catching when in strong sunlight. Most of these plants are hardy; others benefit from a sunny wall.

WALLS, NARROW BORDERS AND WALL SHRUBS

When you are planning to create a path running along the front of a house, and where casement windows open outwards, you should allow for a distance of around 45–60 cm (18–24 in) between the path and wall. This will give you plenty of space for growing a wall shrub, such as *Cotoneaster horizontalis* (Fishbone Cotoneaster), as well as for the window to open and not to obstruct the path.

GLISTENING SEEDHEADS

Climbers with the bonus of silky seedheads in autumn add a further dimension to gardens, especially when the heads are peppered with frost.

However, where a drive abuts a house wall, perhaps on either side of an entrance but where a 30 cm (12 in) wide planting area has been left, pyracanthas are ideal candidates. They can be easily pruned to create eye-catching autumn colour – often extending into winter – at the sides of entrances where they will be readily seen and admired.

Cotoneaster horizontalis *(Fishbone Cotoneaster) is an easily grown wall shrub with masses of red berries in autumn.*

Actinidia chinensis
Chinese Gooseberry UK/USA

Also known as *Actinidia deliciosa*, this deciduous, slightly tender climber has large, heart-shaped, dark green leaves. If male and female flowers are present (usually on separate plants), in warm areas it bears egg-shaped fruits.

Soil and situation: fertile, slightly acid, well-drained but moisture-retentive soil in full sun or partial shade.

Raising new plants: in mid-summer, take 7.5–10 cm (3–4 in) cuttings and insert in pots in gentle warmth.

Cultivation: supports are essential.

↕ 6–7.5 m (20–25 ft) or more ↔ 6–7.5 m (20–25 ft) or more

Celastrus orbiculatus
Bittersweet UK

Hardy, deciduous climber with inconspicuous greenish-yellow flowers, followed in autumn by brown seed capsules that open to reveal bright, orange-yellow and scarlet fruits.

Soil and situation: poor to fairly fertile, moisture-retentive but well-drained soil and a south- or west-facing position in full sun. Avoid chalky soils.

Raising new plants: sow seeds in early winter. Layer young shoots in autumn.

Cultivation: provide support. It will also clamber into trees.

↕ 6–9 m (20–30 ft) ↔ 6–7.5 m (20–25 ft)

Clematis macropetala

Hardy, deciduous, bushy climber with light and dark blue, nodding, bell-shaped flowers in late spring and early summer. These are followed by silvery seedheads.

Soil and situation: fertile, neutral to slightly alkaline, moisture-retentive but well-drained soil in full sun. Shade roots.

Raising new plants: in mid-summer, take 7.5–10 cm (3–4 in) long cuttings and insert in equal parts moist peat and sharp sand in pots. Place them in gentle warmth.

Cultivation: provide support.

↕ 3–3.6 m (10–12 ft) ↔ 1.8–2.4 m (6–8 ft)

Clematis montana
Mountain Clematis UK

Hardy, vigorous, deciduous climber with masses of pure white flowers during late spring and early summer. These are followed by attractive seedheads.

Soil and situation: fertile, neutral to slightly alkaline, moisture-retentive but well-drained soil in full sun. Shade roots.

Raising new plants: in mid-summer, take 7.5–10 cm (3–4 in) long cuttings and insert in equal parts moist peat and sharp sand in pots; place them in gentle warmth.

Cultivation: provide support.

↑ 5.4–7.5 m (18–25 ft) ↔ 5.4–7.5 m (18–25 ft)

Clematis orientalis
Orange-peel Clematis UK

Hardy, vigorous, deciduous climber with nodding, yellow flowers in late summer to mid-autumn. These are followed in autumn by silvery-grey, silky seedheads.

Soil and situation: fertile, neutral to slightly alkaline, moisture-retentive but well-drained soil in full sun. Shade roots.

Raising new plants: during mid-summer, take 7.5–10 cm (3–4 in) long cuttings and insert in equal parts moist peat and sharp sand in pots. Place them in gentle warmth.

Cultivation: provide support.

↑ 3–6 m (10–20 ft) ↔ 3–6 m (10–20 ft)

Clematis vitalba
Old Man's Beard UK

Traveller's Joy UK

Hardy, vigorous, woody climber with a sprawling habit. Green or greenish-white flowers are followed in autumn and winter by masses of silky seedheads.

Soil and situation: deeply prepared, slightly alkaline, well-drained, moisture-retentive soil in full sun or light shade. Shade roots.

Raising new plants: layer low-growing stems.

Cultivation: provide support; it also sprawls over other plants.

↑ 4.5–6 m (15–20 ft) or more ↔ 4.5–6 m (15–20 ft) or more

Cotoneaster horizontalis
Fishbone Cotoneaster UK

Rock Cotoneaster USA

Hardy, deciduous shrub with branches that are initially horizontal but become upright with age. Branches grow in a herringbone-like pattern; in autumn they are smothered in red berries.

Soil and situation: well-drained but moisture-retentive soil in full sun or light shade.

Raising new plants: layer low-growing stems in late summer or autumn.

Cultivation: likes to lean against walls.

↑ 60–90 cm (2–3 ft) ↔ 1.2–1.8 m (4–6 ft)

Passiflora caerulea
Blue Passion Flower USA

Common Passion Flower UK

Slightly tender, deciduous climber with flowers from early to late summer. These are usually followed by yellow fruits.

Soil and situation: poor to moderately fertile, well-drained but moisture-retentive soil and a warm, sheltered position.

Raising new plants: in mid-summer take 7.5–10 cm (3–4 in) long cuttings and insert in pots in gentle warmth.

Cultivation: support is essential.

↑ 1.8–4.5 m (6–15 ft) ↔ 1.8–4.5 m (6–15 ft)

Pyracantha rogersiana 'Flava'
Firethorn UK/USA

Hardy, evergreen shrub with mid-green leaves. In early summer it bears white flowers, followed in autumn, and throughout much of winter, by bright yellow fruits.

Soil and situation: deeply prepared, well-drained soil; full sun or light shade.

Raising new plants: take 7.5–10 cm (3–4 in) long cuttings from the current season's shoots. Insert them in pots and place in gentle warmth.

Cultivation: provide support.

↑ 1.5–2.4 m (5–8 ft) ↔ 1.2–1.8 m (4–6 ft)

Climbing and rambling roses

Do climbers and ramblers vary in size?

The range in vigour and size of climbing and rambling roses is wide, and although some, such as 'Paul's Himalayan Musk', grow to 7.5 m (25 ft) or even higher, 'Pink Perpétué and 'New Dawn' are much lower-growing. Several New English roses are ideal grown as small climbers, as well as shrubs in borders. You should always choose a climber or rambler to suit the space available, and the way it is to be grown. There are many roses to choose from.

SAY IT WITH ROSES!

A few climbing and rambling roses have romantic names that offer amusing and remindful messages for courting couples. 'Compassion' is a Modern climber with salmon-pink flowers that are tinted apricot-orange, as well as a beautiful fragrance, and 'Dream Girl' is a climbing rose with coral-pink, spicily fragrant flowers. 'Hero' is a New English Rose with glistening pink, richly fragrant flowers. 'New Dawn' is another Modern climber, which produces clusters of silvery blush-pink flowers that deepen towards their centres. It also has a fresh and fruity fragrance. 'Wedding Day' is a rambling rose with a vigorous growth habit and large clusters of flowers; they are apricot-coloured when in bud, opening to creamy-yellow and turning to white. It is also delightfully scented.

Roses are ideal for adorning recessed statuary. However, choose a colour that does not dominate the statue.

THORNLESS ROSES

Climbers and ramblers with few or no thorns are ideal for gardens where children play or people with sight problems walk.

These roses include 'Kathleen Harrop' (see page 44), 'Veilchenblau' (see page 47) and 'Zéphirine Drouhin' (see page 47).

'Adélaïde d'Orléans'

Sempervirens-type rambler with almost evergreen foliage. In mid-summer it bears small, semi-double, creamy-pink flowers with a primrose-like fragrance.

Soil and situation: fertile, moisture-retentive but well-drained neutral or slightly acid soil in good light and where air can freely circulate around branches and stems.

Raising new plants: buy plants from a specialist nursery.

Cultivation: ideal for walls, arches and pergolas.

↕ 3.6–4.5 m (12–15 ft) ↔ 1.5–2.1 m (5–7 ft)

'Aimée Vibert'

Noisette-type climber with a bushy nature and graceful sprays of small, double, pure white flowers with a musk-like fragrance during late summer and early autumn.

Soil and situation: fertile, moisture-retentive but well-drained neutral or slightly acid soil in good light and where air can freely circulate around branches and stems.

Raising new plants: buy plants from a specialist nursery.

Cultivation: it can be grown as a shrub as well as a climber against a wall.

↕ 3.6–4.5 m (12–15 ft) ↔ 3 m (10 ft)

'Albéric Barbier'

Wichuraiana-type rambler with a vigorous nature and small, yellow buds in early and mid-summer that open into large, double, creamy-white flowers with a fruity fragrance.

Soil and situation: fertile, moisture-retentive, well-drained neutral or slightly acid soil in good light and where air can freely circulate around the stems.

Raising new plants: buy plants from a specialist nursery.

Cultivation: ideal for covering walls, growing into trees and clothing arches and pergolas.

↕ 4.5–6 m (15–20 ft) ↔ 3.6–4.5 m (12–15 ft)

'Albertine'
Wichuraiana-type rambler with almost double, fragrant, light salmon-pink flowers; it is not repeat-flowering but is very floriferous.

Soil and situation: fertile, moisture-retentive but well-drained neutral or slightly acid soil in good light and where air can freely circulate around branches and stems.

Raising new plants: buy plants from a specialist nursery.

Cultivation: ideal for covering an arch or pergola, or clambering into a tree.

↕ 4.5–5.4 m (15–18 ft) ↔ 3.6–4.5 m (12–15 ft)

'Alexandre Girault'
Wichuraiana-type rambler with fragrant, reddish-pink flowers that become flat and quartered and assume a lilac-carmine shade, with a hint of yellow at each petal's base.

Soil and situation: fertile, moisture-retentive but well-drained neutral or slightly acid soil in good light and where air can freely circulate around branches and stems.

Raising new plants: buy plants from a specialist nursery.

Cultivation: it is old-fashioned in nature and is ideal for covering a large trellis or pergola.

↕ 4.5–6 m (15–20 ft) ↔ 3.6–4.5 m (12–15 ft)

'Alister Stella Gray'
Noisette-type climber with clusters of fragrant, fully double, rosette-shaped, pale yellow and orange-centred flowers. It is repeat-flowering.

Soil and situation: fertile, moisture-retentive but well-drained neutral or slightly acid soil in good light and where air can freely circulate around branches and stems.

Raising new plants: buy plants from a specialist nursery.

Cultivation: it can be used to clothe a wall, or as a shrub in a border.

↕ 4.5 m (15 ft) ↔ 3 m (10 ft)

'Aloha'
Modern climber, with a short and often bushy nature. It is a large-flowered type, with cupped, fragrant, clear-pink flowers, and is repeat-flowering.

Soil and situation: fertile, moisture-retentive but well-drained neutral or slightly acid soil in good light and where air can freely circulate around branches and stems.

Raising new plants: buy plants from a specialist nursery.

Cultivation: plant it against a wall, grow it as a shrub in a border, or use it to clothe a tripod or pillar.

↕ 2.4 m (8 ft) ↔ 2.4 m (8 ft)

'Bobbie James'
Multiflora hybrid with a rambling habit and fragrant, semi-double, creamy-white flowers with bright yellow stamens in mid-summer. It has a informal look.

Soil and situation: fertile, moisture-retentive but well-drained neutral or slightly acid soil in good light and where air can freely circulate around branches and stems.

Raising new plants: buy plants from a specialist nursery.

Cultivation: it is ideal for clambering into trees, covering a pergola and for screening unsightly buildings.

↕ 6–7.5 m (20–25 ft) ↔ 6–7.5 m (20–25 ft)

'Climbing Cécile Brünner'
Vigorous climbing sport of a China Rose, with beautifully shaped, thimble-sized, double, slightly fragrant, shell-pink flowers during mid-summer.

Soil and situation: fertile, moisture-retentive but well-drained neutral or slightly acid soil in good light and where air can freely circulate around branches and stems.

Raising new plants: buy plants from a specialist nursery.

Cultivation: it can be grown against a wall, or allowed to clamber into trees.

↕ 3.6–5.4 m (12–18 ft) ↔ 3.6–5.4 m (12–18 ft)

'Climbing Crimson Glory'

Climbing sport of a popular Hybrid Tea rose, with a stiff and branching nature and fragrant, deep crimson flowers in early summer. Occasionally, it makes a repeat flowering.

Soil and situation: fertile, moisture-retentive but well-drained neutral or slightly acid soil in good light and where air can freely circulate around branches and stems.

Raising new plants: buy plants from a specialist nursery.

Cultivation: it is ideal for clothing walls and as a pillar rose.

↕ 3.6–4.5 m (12–15 ft) ↔ 2.1–2.8 m (7–8 ft)

'Climbing Étoile de Hollande'

Climbing sport of a popular Hybrid Tea rose. It bears very fragrant, loosely formed, double, dark red flowers. After its first flush of flowers it repeats in late summer.

Soil and situation: fertile, moisture-retentive but well-drained neutral or slightly acid soil in good light and where air can freely circulate around branches and stems.

Raising new plants: buy plants from a specialist nursery.

Cultivation: ideal for clothing walls.

↕ 4.5–5.4 m (15–18 ft) ↔ 3.6–4.5 m (12–15 ft)

'Climbing Lady Sylvia'

Climbing sport of a Hybrid Tea rose, with very fragrant, double, pale pink flowers with yellow bases. It flowers during late summer.

Soil and situation: fertile, moisture-retentive but well-drained neutral or slightly acid soil in good light and where air can freely circulate around branches and stems.

Raising new plants: buy plants from a specialist nursery.

Cultivation: it is ideal for planting against a wall.

↕ 3.6 m (12 ft) ↔ 2.4–3 m (8–10 ft)

'Climbing Lady Hillingdon'

Vigorous climbing sport of a well-known Tea Rose. It is freely branching, with large, richly scented, semi-double, apricot-yellow flowers throughout much of summer.

Soil and situation: fertile, moisture-retentive but well-drained neutral or slightly acid soil in good light and where air can freely circulate around branches and stems. It needs a warm position.

Raising new plants: buy plants from a specialist nursery.

Cultivation: it is ideal for clothing a sun-warmed wall.

↕ 3.6–4.5 m (12–15 ft) ↔ 2.1–2.4 m (7–8 ft)

'Constance Spry'

Superb New English Rose with large, paeony-shaped, clear rose-pink flowers with a strong myrrh-like fragrance mainly during early summer. The flowers appear on somewhat nodding stems.

Soil and situation: fertile, moisture-retentive but well-drained neutral or slightly acid soil in good light and where air can freely circulate around branches and stems.

Raising new plants: buy plants from a specialist nursery.

Cultivation: it can be grown as a shrub, as well as a climber.

↕ 1.8–3 m (6–10 ft) ↔ 1.8–2.1 m (6–7 ft)

'Crimson Shower'

Wichuraiana rambler, with dense clusters of small, semi-double, bright crimson flowers in mid-summer until early autumn. It has rather lax growth.

Soil and situation: fertile, moisture-retentive but well-drained neutral or slightly acid soil in good light and where air can freely circulate around branches and stems.

Raising new plants: buy plants from a specialist nursery.

Cultivation: it is ideal for clothing trellises, arches and pillars.

↕ 2.1–3 m (7–10 ft) ↔ 1.8–2.1 m (6–7 ft)

'Danse du Feu'

Modern climber, with clusters of semi-double, globular, brilliant orange-scarlet flowers, but little scent. It is repeat-flowering.

Soil and situation: fertile, moisture-retentive but well-drained neutral or slightly acid soil in good light and where air can freely circulate around branches and stems.

Raising new plants: buy plants from a specialist nursery.

Cultivation: it is ideal for clothing walls, especially cold ones.

⬆ 2.4–3 m (8–10 ft) ⬌ 1.8–2.4 m (6–8 ft)

'François Juranville'

Wichuaraiana-type rambler with small clusters of double, coral-pink flowers and a sharp and apple-like fragrance in early and mid-summer.

Soil and situation: fertile, moisture-retentive but well-drained neutral or slightly acid soil in good light and where air can freely circulate around branches and stems.

Raising new plants: buy plants from a specialist nursery.

Cultivation: it is ideal for clothing a pergola or arch.

⬆ 4.5–6 m (15–20 ft) ⬌ 4.5–6 m (15–20 ft)

'Gerbe Rose'

Wichuraiana-type rambler with large clusters of double, quartered, pink flowers with a delicious paeony-like fragrance during mid-summer, and again later. Flowers are tinted cream and borne on stiff stems.

Soil and situation: fertile, moisture-retentive but well-drained neutral or slightly acid soil in good light and where air can freely circulate around branches and stems.

Raising new plants: buy plants from a specialist nursery.

Cultivation: it is ideal for planting as a pillar rose.

⬆ 3–3.6 m (10–12 ft) ⬌ 2.4–3 m (8–10 ft)

'Gloire de Dijon'

Noisette-type climber that is both early- and repeat-flowering. It develops medium to large, double, quartered, buff-yellow, fragrant flowers.

Soil and situation: fertile, moisture-retentive but well-drained neutral or slightly acid soil in good light and where air can freely circulate around branches and stems.

Raising new plants: buy plants from a specialist nursery.

Cultivation: it is ideal for planting against a wall.

⬆ 3.6–4.5 m (12–15 ft) ⬌ 3–3.6 m (10–12 ft)

'Golden Showers'

A Modern climber that flowers freely and continuously. It bears clusters of fragrant, large, semi-double, bright yellow flowers throughout much of summer and until the frosts of autumn.

Soil and situation: fertile, moisture-retentive but well-drained neutral or slightly acid soil in good light and where air can freely circulate around branches and stems. Ideal for a cold wall.

Raising new plants: buy plants from a specialist nursery.

Cultivation: ideal as a pillar rose, against a wall, as a shrub in a border.

⬆ 2.4–3 m (8–10 ft) ⬌ 1.8 m (6 ft)

'Guinée'

Climber with strong growth and large, double, scented, very dark red flowers borne mainly during early summer. It is repeat-flowering. The flowers often have the appearance of black shading.

Soil and situation: fertile, moisture-retentive but well-drained neutral or slightly acid soil in good light and where air can freely circulate.

Raising new plants: buy plants from a specialist nursery.

Cultivation: it is best grown against a light-coloured wall.

⬆ 3–4.5 m (10–15 ft) ⬌ 1.8–2.4 m (6–8 ft)

'Kathleen Harrop'

Climbing Bourbon rose, with clusters of fragrant, light pink, medium to large semi-double flowers throughout much of summer. It has an arching habit and thornless stems.

Soil and situation: fertile, moisture-retentive but well-drained neutral or slightly acid soil in good light and where air can freely circulate.

Raising new plants: buy plants from a specialist nursery.

Cultivation: it is ideal for growing as a pillar rose.

↕ 3 m (10 ft) ↔ 2.1–2.4 m (7–8 ft)

'Leverkusen'

Kordesii-type, hardy climber that bears rosette-shaped, lemon-yellow flowers with a distinctive lemon-like fragrance during mid-summer, and again later.

Soil and situation: fertile, moisture-retentive but well-drained neutral or slightly acid soil in good light and where air can freely circulate around branches and stems.

Raising new plants: buy plants from a specialist nursery.

Cultivation: it is ideal for covering a wall, as well as for growing as a pillar rose and as a shrub in a border.

↕ 3 m (10 ft) ↔ 1.8–2.4 m (6–8 ft)

'Madame Alfred Carrière'

Noisette-type climber, with clusters of double, cupped, richly fragrant, white flowers with a blush tint. It is free- and repeat-flowering.

Soil and situation: fertile, moisture-retentive but well-drained neutral or slightly acid soil in good light and where air can freely circulate around branches and stems.

Raising new plants: buy plants from a specialist nursery.

Cultivation: it is ideal for clothing a wall, even a cold one.

↕ 4.5–5.4 m (15–18 ft) ↔ 3 m (10 ft)

'Madame Grégoire Staechelin'

Large-flowered climber with buds that open to reveal semi-double, coral-pink flowers in early summer. They are about 13 cm (5 in) across and with a delicate Sweet Pea-like fragrance.

Soil and situation: fertile, moisture-retentive but well-drained neutral or slightly acid soil in good light and where air can freely circulate around branches and stems.

Raising new plants: buy plants from a specialist nursery.

Cultivation: superb against a wall.

↕ 4.5–6 m (15–20 ft) ↔ 3.6–5.4 m (12–18 ft)

'Maigold'

Climber with large, fragrant, semi-double, bronze-yellow flowers with golden stamens during early summer. However, take care as the stems are sharply thorned. Removing dead flowers helps to encourage the development of further flowers.

Soil and situation: fertile, moisture-retentive, well-drained neutral or slightly acid soil in good light and where air can freely circulate around stems.

Raising new plants: buy plants from a specialist nursery.

Cultivation: superb against a wall.

↕ 2.4–3 m (8–10 ft) ↔ 2.4–3 m (8–10 ft)

'Meg'

Large-flowered climber with clusters of fragrant, flattish, semi-double, light apricot-pink flowers during early and mid-summer, and often again later.

Soil and situation: fertile, moisture-retentive but well-drained neutral or slightly acid soil in good light and where air can freely circulate around branches and stems.

Raising new plants: buy plants from a specialist nursery.

Cultivation: ideal for a wall, pergola or pillar.

↕ 3–3.6 m (10–12 ft) ↔ 3–3.6 m (10–12 ft)

'Mermaid'

Vigorous, large-flowered climber, with fragrant, large, single, primrose-yellow flowers with amber-coloured stamens. It is repeat-flowering.

Soil and situation: fertile, moisture-retentive but well-drained neutral or slightly acid soil in good light and where air can freely circulate around branches and stems. It requires a warm wall.

Raising new plants: buy plants from a specialist nursery.

Cultivation: ideal for growing against a warm, sunny wall.

↑ 5.4–6 m (18–20 ft) ↔ 5.4–6 m (18–20 ft)

'New Dawn'

Climber with a bushy habit and big sprays of fragrant, small to medium-sized, double, silvery blush-pink flowers that are borne almost continuously throughout summer.

Soil and situation: fertile, moisture-retentive but well-drained neutral or slightly acid soil in good light and where air can freely circulate around branches and stems.

Raising new plants: buy plants from a specialist nursery.

Cultivation: ideal for growing against a wall or as a pillar.

↑ 3 m (10 ft) ↔ 2.4 m (8 ft)

'Noisette Carnée'

Also known as 'Blush Noisette', this is the original Noisette rose. It has clusters of small, cupped, semi-double, lilac-pink flowers with a rich clove-like fragrance throughout summer.

Soil and situation: fertile, moisture-retentive but well-drained neutral or slightly acid soil in good light and where air can freely circulate around branches and stems.

Raising new plants: buy plants from a specialist nursery.

Cultivation: it can be grown as a shrub as well as a climber.

↑ 2.4–3 m (8–10 ft) ↔ 2.4–3 m (8–10 ft)

'Paul's Himalayan Musk'

Vigorous rambler, with spectacular sprays of small, double, blush to lilac-pink flowers. It has long, trailing, thin stems that enable the flowers to hang down.

Soil and situation: fertile, moisture-retentive but well-drained neutral or slightly acid soil in good light and where air can freely circulate around branches and stems. It needs plenty of space.

Raising new plants: buy plants from a specialist nursery.

Cultivation: it is ideal for growing into trees, as well as clothing large pergolas.

↑ 7.5–9 m (25–30 ft) ↔ 6–7.5 m (20–25 ft)

'Paul Transon'

Wichuraiana-type rambler, which produces medium to small clusters of strongly apple-scented, coppery-orange flowers. It is repeat-flowering, especially in warm seasons.

Soil and situation: fertile, moisture-retentive but well-drained neutral or slightly acid soil in good light and where air can freely circulate around branches and stems.

Raising new plants: buy plants from a specialist nursery.

Cultivation: it is ideal for pillars and small pergolas.

↑ 3 m (10 ft) ↔ 2.4 m (8 ft)

'Pink Perpétué'

Large-flowered Modern climber, with large clusters of pink flowers with carmine reverses. It is both free- and repeat-flowering.

Soil and situation: fertile, moisture-retentive but well-drained neutral or slightly acid soil in good light and where air can freely circulate around branches and stems.

Raising new plants: buy plants from a specialist nursery.

Cultivation: it is ideal for clothing a pillar or an arch.

↑ 2.4–3.6 m (8–12 ft) ↔ 2.1–2.4 m (7–8 ft)

'Rambling Rector'

Multiflora rambler with strong, twiggy growth and clusters of fragrant, creamy-white flowers with golden stamens. It is not repeat-flowering, but in autumn produces small hips (fruits).

Soil and situation: fertile, moisture-retentive but well-drained neutral or slightly acid soil in good light and where air can freely circulate around branches and stems.

Raising new plants: buy plants from a specialist nursery.

Cultivation: ideal for pergolas, as well as forming a dense shrub in a border.

↕ 4.5–6 m (15–20 ft) ↔ 4.5–5.4 m (15–18 ft)

'Rêve d'Or'

Climbing Noisette type, with an informal nature and slightly fragrant, semi-double, buff-yellow flowers with pink shading. It is repeat-flowering.

Soil and situation: fertile, moisture-retentive but well-drained neutral or slightly acid soil in good light and where air can freely circulate around branches and stems.

Raising new plants: buy plants from a specialist nursery.

Cultivation: ideal for growing against a wall.

↕ 3–3.6 m (10–12 ft) ↔ 2.4–3 m (8–10 ft)

'Sander's White Rambler'

Sometimes known as 'Sander's White', this Wichuraiana rambler bears clusters of fragrant, small, double, rosette-type, white flowers on arching and trailing stems. It flowers during mid-summer, and is not repeat-flowering.

Soil and situation: fertile, moisture-retentive but well-drained neutral or slightly acid soil in good light and where air can freely circulate around branches and stems.

Raising new plants: buy plants from a specialist nursery.

Cultivation: ideal on walls, as well as clothing pillars and arches.

↕ 3.6–4.5 m (12–15 ft) ↔ 3–3.6 m (10–12 ft)

'Shropshire Lass'

English rose type of climber, with superb myrrh-like fragrance, and large, flat, semi-double, delicate pink flowers fading to white in early summer. It has a prominent bunch of stamens.

Soil and situation: fertile, moisture-retentive but well-drained neutral or slightly acid soil in good light and where air can freely circulate around branches and stems.

Raising new plants: buy plants from a specialist nursery.

Cultivation: ideal for planting against walls, as well as a shrub in a border.

↕ 3–3.6 m (10–12 ft) ↔ 1.8–2.4 m (6–8 ft)

'St Swithun'

Climbing English rose, with large, cupped, soft pink flowers fading to white at their edges, and with a strong myrrh-like fragrance.

Soil and situation: fertile, moisture-retentive but well-drained neutral or slightly acid soil in good light and where air can freely circulate around branches and stems.

Raising new plants: buy plants from a specialist nursery.

Cultivation: ideal for planting against walls, as well as a shrub in a border.

↕ 1.8–2.4 m (6–8 ft) ↔ 1.5–2.1 m (5–7 ft)

'The Garland'

Beautiful old rambler with bunches of semi-double, white to blush flowers with a superb orange fragrance during mid-summer. The growth is rather twiggy and, in autumn, bears red hips (fruits).

Soil and situation: fertile, moisture-retentive but well-drained neutral or slightly acid soil in good light and where air can freely circulate around branches and stems.

Raising new plants: buy plants from a specialist nursery.

Cultivation: can be grown against a wall, as well as a shrub in a border.

↕ 3.6–4.5 m (12–15 ft) ↔ 3 m (10 ft)

'Veilchenblau'

Multiflora-type rambler with massed bunches of small, dark magenta, semi-double flowers with a rich orange fragrance during mid-summer. The flowers fade to lilac and are sometimes streaked with white.

Soil and situation: fertile, moisture-retentive but well-drained neutral or slightly acid soil in good light and where air can freely circulate around branches and stems.

Raising new plants: buy plants from a specialist nursery.

Cultivation: it is ideal for growing up a pillar or clothing an arch or pergola.

⬍ 4.5 m (15 ft) ⬌ 3.6 m (12 ft)

'Wedding Day'

Vigorous rambler with clusters of scented, creamy-white to blush, small and single flowers with yellow stamens. It flowers in mid-summer, and in autumn bears small, yellowish hips (fruits).

Soil and situation: fertile, moisture-retentive but well-drained neutral or slightly acid soil in good light and where air can freely circulate around branches and stems.

Raising new plants: buy plants from a specialist nursery.

Cultivation: it is ideal for clambering into large trees.

⬍ 6–7.5 m (10–25 ft) ⬌ 3.6 m (12 ft)

'Zéphirine Drouhin'

Bourbon-type climber with masses of deep rose-pink flowers with a sweet and penetrating fragrance during early summer, and again later.

Soil and situation: fertile, moisture-retentive but well-drained neutral or slightly acid soil in good light and where air can freely circulate around branches and stems.

Raising new plants: buy plants from a specialist nursery.

Cultivation: ideal as a climber against a shaded, cold wall, as well as being grown as a shrub in a border.

⬍ 1.8–2.7 m (6–9 ft) ⬌ 1.5–2.4 m (5–8 ft)

OTHER CLIMBING AND RAMBLING ROSES

There is a wealth of climbing and rambling roses available in addition to the ones illustrated on pages 40–47, and these include the following:

- **'Auguste Gervais' (Wichuraiana rambling rose):** 6 m (20 ft) high; the coppery-yellow and salmon flowers are packed with short petals and open to a flat formation. It has a delightful fragrance.
- **'Céline Forestier' (Noisette climber):** 2.4 m (8 ft) high; the beautiful, full-petalled, pale yellow flowers have a Tea Rose fragrance and old-rose formation.
- **'Compassion' (Modern climber):** 3 m (10 ft) high; the salmon-pink flowers are tinted with apricot-orange and give off a sweet fragrance. The flowers have a Hybrid Tea rose shape.
- **'Dream Girl' (climber):** 3 m (10 ft) high; this rose bears coral-pink, spicily fragrant flowers. Each flower has a beautiful rosette shape.
- **'Félicité et Perpétue' (Sempervirens rambler):** 6 m (20 ft) high; it produces large clusters of pompon-like, creamy-white flowers that give off a very delicate, primrose-like fragrance.
- **'Francis E. Lester' (rambler with Hybrid Musk parentage):** 4.5 m (15 ft) high; this rose produces large clusters of white flowers, tinted blush at their edges, as well as a strong fragrance. Additionally, it bears masses of orange fruits (hips or heps) in autumn.

- **'Graham Thomas' (New English rose):** 1.8–2.4 m (6–8 ft) high; although often grown as a bush rose, it is also superb as a climber. It bears rich yellow flowers with a strong Tea Rose fragrance.
- **'Hero' (New English climbing rose):** 2.1–2.4 m (7–8 ft) high; this rose has beautiful, glistening-pink flowers with a rich fragrance and a cupped and open shape. Although it can be grown as a straggly bush rose, it performs better as a climber.
- **'Lawrence Johnston' (climber):** 6–7.5 m (20–25 ft) high; the large, semi-double, clear yellow flowers have a strong fragrance.
- **'Leander' (New English climbing rose):** 3–3.6 m (10–12 ft) high; this plant bears sprays of deep apricot, small flowers with a superb raspberry-like fragrance. It can also be grown as a bush rose.
- **'Mistress Quickly' (New English climbing rose):** 2.4–3 m (8–10 ft) high; the small, pink flowers of this climber are borne in pretty sprays. It can also be grown as a bush rose.
- **'Snow Goose' (New English climbing rose):** 1.8–2.4 m (6–8 ft) high; the small, white, pompon-like flowers have a musk-like fragrance.
- **'Weetwood' (rambler):** 6–7.5 m (20–25 ft) high; it has sprays of pink flowers with an old-fashioned appearance. Each flower is about 6 cm (2½ in) wide.

Covering walls

Which climbers cover walls best?

The choice of plants for covering walls is extensive, ranging from flowering climbers to those with evergreen and perhaps variegated leaves, as well as deciduous types with leaves that assume rich colours before falling in autumn. There are also colourful and floriferous roses (see opposite page). Some roses need a sunny wall, while others create magnificent displays on cold and exposed sites. There are also roses that will grow well even in poor soils.

INSPIRATION FOR YOUR WALLS

Autumn-coloured climbers create dominant feasts of colour.

Ivies will soon clothe walls and eyesores.

Passiflora caerulea (Common Passion Flower) bears colourful and intricately formed flowers.

Many roses are superb for covering walls in colourful flowers.

Wisteria is vigorous and soon clothes a wall, but will need regular pruning.

Climbers can be used to create attractive screens and divisions in gardens.

CLIMBERS FOR WALLS

Flowering climbers for walls

- *Clematis* – large-flowered hybrids – see pages 27–28.
- *Jasminum officinale* (Common White Jasmine) – see page 29.
- *Lapageria rosea* (Chilean Bell Flower) – see page 29.
- *Trachelospermum jasminoides* (Star Jasmine) – see page 31.
- *Wisteria floribunda* (Japanese Wisteria) – see page 31.

Coloured foliage

- *Actinidia kolomikta* (Kolomikta Vine) – see page 34.
- *Hedera canariensis* 'Gloire de Marengo' (Variegated Canary Island Ivy) – see page 34.
- *Hedera colchica* 'Sulphur Heart' – see page 35.
- *Hedera helix* 'Goldheart' – see page 35.
- *Humulus lupulus* 'Aureus' (Golden-leaved Hop) – see page 35.
- *Jasminum officinale* 'Aureum' – see page 35.

Autumn-coloured leaves

- *Celastrus orbiculatus* (Climbing Bittersweet) – see page 36.
- *Parthenocissus quinquefolia* (Virginia Creeper) – see page 36.
- *Parthenocissus tricuspidata* (Boston Ivy) – see page 37.
- *Vitis coignetiae* (Crimson Glory Vine) – see page 37.

WALL SHRUBS TO CONSIDER

Some wall shrubs are hardy, others slightly tender.

Extremely hardy wall shrubs:

- *Cotoneaster horizontalis* (Fishbone Cotoneaster) – see page 39.
- *Pyracantha rogersiana* (Firethorn) – see page 39.

Slightly tender wall shrubs:

- *Abutilon megapotamicum* – see page 24.
- *Azara microphylla* – see page 25.
- *Carpenteria californica* (Tree Anemone) – see page 25.

Supports for climbers

Strong trellises and sound wall-fixings (anchors) are essential for climbers that require support. See pages 12–13 for climbers that need support, and for how to erect a trellis.

DAMAGE TO WALLS

Climbers that have suckers and aerial roots may penetrate brickwork and cause damage, especially to loose bricks and aged pebble-dashed (stoned) walls. Make sure that all surfaces are sound.

These climbers (especially ivies) become drenched in dust. Therefore, use a face mask and protective glasses when cutting them back.

Roses for especially warm walls

- 'Aimée Vibert': climber – see page 40.
- 'Climbing Étoile de Hollande': climber – see page 42.
- 'Climbing Lady Hillingdon': climber – see page 42.
- 'Mermaid': climber – see page 45.
- 'The Garland': rambler – see page 46.

Roses for cold walls

- 'Albéric Barbier': rambler – see page 40.
- 'Gloire de Dijon': climber – see page 43.
- 'Golden Showers': climber – see page 43.
- 'Madame Grégoire Staechelin': climber – see page 44.
- 'New Dawn': climber – see page 45.
- 'Zéphirine Drouhin': climber – see page 47.

Roses for poor conditions

- 'Climbing Cécile Brünner': climber – see page 41.
- 'Constance Spry': climber – see page 42.
- 'Leverkusen': climber – see page 44.
- 'Madame Alfred Carrière': climber – see page 44.
- 'Noisette Carnée' (also known as 'Blush Noisette'): climber – see page 45.

Dressing pergolas

There are several types of pergola. Some are informal and are constructed from rustic poles; others are more formal and include the use of planed timber (lumber). The traditional type has cross-beams formed of squared timber (lumber) with straight-cut ends. However, the oriental type uses cross-beams about 5 cm (2 in) wide and 15 cm (6 in) deep, with their ends chamfered on the undersides. There are also lean-to pergolas; these are invariably formal in nature.

What is a pergola?

Leafy climbers help to create cloistered corners in gardens. Deciduous, large-leaved climbers are usually the best choice for this situation.

Roses for pergolas

- 'Albéric Barbier' (rambler) – see page 40.
- 'Albertine' (rambler) – see page 41.
- 'Crimson Shower' (rambler) – see page 42.
- 'François Juranville' (rambler) – see page 43.
- 'Veilchenblau' (rambler) – see page 47.

Roses for tripods and pillars

- 'Aloha' (Modern climber) – see page 41.
- 'Golden Showers' (Modern climber) – see page 43.
- 'Leverkusen' (climber) – see page 44.
- 'Maigold' (climber) – see page 44.
- 'Pink Perpétué' (Modern climber) – see page 45.

CLIMBERS FOR PERGOLAS

- *Jasminum officinale* (Common White Jasmine) – see page 29.
- *Lonicera periclymenum* 'Belgica' (Early Dutch Honeysuckle) – see page 30.
- *Lonicera periclymenum* 'Serotina' (Late Dutch Honeysuckle) – see page 30.
- *Vitis coignetiae* (Crimson Glory Vine) – see page 37.
- *Vitis vinifera* 'Purpurea' (Teinturier Grape) – see page 37.
- *Wisteria floribunda* (Japanese Wisteria) – see page 31.
- *Wisteria sinensis* (Chinese Wisteria) – see page 31.

PILLARS AND TRIPODS

A pillar is formed of a strong piece of conifer trunk, and a tripod is made of planed timber (lumber), both 2.1–2.4 m (7–8 ft) in height.

How to make a small lean-to pergola

Construct a small, lean-to pergola against a wall to create a plant-covered leisure area. Concrete the base of each vertical post in a 60 cm (2 ft) deep hole. Secure cross-timbers (beams) to wall-brackets (anchors); a traditional, formal design is best. Use a builder's spirit-level (carpenter's level) to check that the posts are upright and the main beam is level.

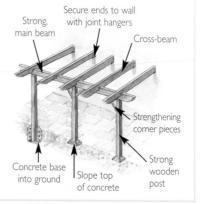

Strong, main beam

Secure ends to wall with joint hangers

Cross-beam

Strengthening corner pieces

Concrete base into ground

Slope top of concrete

Strong wooden post

Clothing arches and tunnels

Arches over paths are spectacular, especially when clad in beautiful flowering or leafy climbers. Roses can be used, but remember that people with limited vision might be harmed by rose stems that are insufficiently secured and able to trail or be blown in the wind. In such circumstances, flowering climbers are often the better choice, especially those with unusual and distinctive fragrances. A series of arches can also be used to create a tunnel.

Are arches hard to clothe?

FRAGRANT ROSES FOR ARCHES

Arches prettily dressed in flowering climbers are idyllic.

There are many suitable roses for training on arches, and some are exquisitely fragrant. Remember, however, that you must select the vigour of the rose to suit the size of the arch.
- **'Albéric Barbier' (rambler):** bears fruity-scented, creamy-white flowers – see page 40.
- **'Albertine' (rambler):** has strongly scented, salmon-pink flowers – see page 41.
- **'François Juranville' (rambler):** has an apple-like fragrance, and coral-pink flowers – see page 43.
- **'Veilchenblau' (rambler):** bears richly orange-scented, dark magenta flowers fading to lilac, and occasionally streaked with white – see page 47.

LABURNUM TUNNELS

These are spectacular and need to be high and wide to enable the 25–30 cm (10–12 in) long clusters of yellow flowers to hang freely during late spring and early summer. Use a series of metal arches and connecting wires as the basic framework (see above right).

Starting 1.2 m (4 ft) from the end of the tunnel, plant *Laburnum* x *watereri* 'Vossii' at 2.4 m (8 ft) intervals along each side. Initially, train stems upright, at the same time taking lateral shoots along the supporting framework.

Laburnum responds well to spur pruning; in winter, prune shoots that are growing inwards or away from the frame, cutting them back to three buds. Cut back lateral shoots when they fill the allotted space, and tie in and train the main vertical shoots over the frame.

Creating a fully clothed, flowering laburnum tunnel takes several years.

Annual climbers for small arches

- *Cobaea scandens* (Cathedral Bells): velvety-purple flowers – see page 32.
- *Ipomoea purpurea* (Common Morning Glory): large purple flowers – see page 32.
- *Lathyrus odoratus* (Sweet Pea): wide colour range – see page 33.
- *Thunbergia alata* (Black-eyed Susan): white, orange or yellow flowers with a characteristic chocolate-brown eye – see page 33.
- *Tropaeolum majus* (Nasturtium): wide colour range – see page 33.
- *Tropaeolum peregrinum* (Canary Creeper): canary-yellow flowers – see page 33.

A mature laburnum tunnel is a stunning feature

Rustic arches are ideal for informal gardens

Wrought-iron arches have a casual look

Arches over gates are memorable for visitors

How to make a classic pergola-topped arch

Add an Oriental quality to the top of an arch by chamfering or ornately shaping the lower ends of the cross-timbers (beams). The ends of these timbers (beams) should protrude 23–30 cm (9–12 in) from the arch's sides.

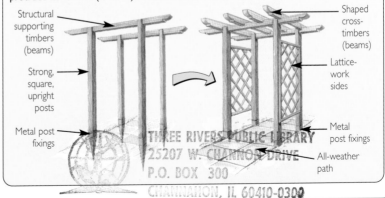

Structural supporting timbers (beams)

Strong, square, upright posts

Metal post fixings

Shaped cross-timbers (beams)

Lattice-work sides

Metal post fixings

All-weather path

Arbours

Are arbours easy to clothe?

There is a good choice of flowering and leafy climbers, as well as roses, that are suitable for clothing an arbour, where they create a private and cloistered area. Aim to create a shady retreat, with a latticework frame covered in climbing plants. Trees and shrubs can be used to form the sides, with the possibility of positioning the arbour against an established hedge. Adding fragrant climbers gives the arbour a further and much-treasured quality.

Arbours that are drenched in rich fragrances create oases of rest and tranquillity in a secluded part of the garden.

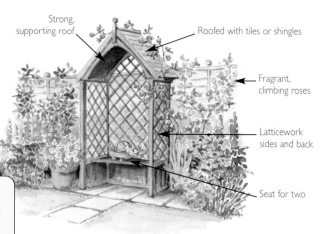

Strong, supporting roof

Roofed with tiles or shingles

Fragrant, climbing roses

Latticework sides and back

Seat for two

Self-assembled or ready-made arbours can be used to create attractive focal points at the end of a garden quickly and simply.

Flowering climbers for arbours

Fragrant climbers introduce romance to arbours, drenching them in sweet as well as usual redolences, including vanilla and hawthorn. Here are a few flowering climbers to consider.

- *Clematis flammula* (Fragrant Virgin's Bower) – page 26.
- *Clematis montana* (Mountain Clematis) – see page 27.
- *Jasminum officinale* (Common White Jasmine) – see page 29.
- *Lonicera periclymenum* 'Belgica' (Early Dutch Honeysuckle) – see page 30.
- *Lonicera periclymenum* 'Serotina' (Late Dutch Honeysuckle) – see page 30.
- *Wisteria floribunda* (Japanese Wisteria) – see page 31.
- *Wisteria sinensis* (Chinese Wisteria) – see page 31.

Leafy climbers for arbours

Some leaf-drenched climbers create a covering of large leaves at head height and can be used to form an attractive canopy for an arbour. They help to keep the bower cool and shaded from midday sun. Here are a few deciduous climbers to consider, with the bonus of gloriously coloured leaves in autumn.

- *Vitis amurensis* (Amurland Grape) – see page 37.
- *Vitis coignetiae* (Crimson Glory Vine) – see page 37.
- *Vitis vinifera* 'Purpurea' (Teinturier Grape) – see page 37.

Roses for arbours

Both climbing and rambling roses can be used to clothe arbours, although ramblers with their pliable and adaptable stems are better for creating overhead colour and fragrance. Here are a few ramblers to consider.

- 'Albéric Barbier': fruity-scented, creamy-white flowers – see page 40.
- 'Albertine': strongly scented, salmon-pink flowers – see page 41.
- 'Crimson Shower': bright crimson flowers – see page 42.
- 'François Juranville': apple-like fragrance, coral-pink flowers – see page 43.
- 'Veilchenblau': richly orange-scented, dark magenta flowers fading to lilac and occasionally streaked with white – see page 47.

Many colourful roses that are suitable for arbours are richly fragrant.

Free-standing screens

Free-standing screens – usually trellis – are ideal for separating parts of a garden and for blocking views to and from neighbouring gardens. They can also be used in front gardens to create head-height privacy close to boundaries formed of 90 cm (3 ft) high fences. Do not position free-standing screens closer than 75 cm (2½ ft) to a boundary, however, as trailing stems might intrude on a neighbour's garden. Flowering and leafy climbers, as well as roses, can be used.

Why use free-standing screens?

Flowering climbers for free-standing screens

The range of climbers for growing over a free-standing screen is wide and includes many with appealing fragrances. Here are some climbers to consider.

- *Clematis chrysocoma* – see page 26.
- *Clematis flammula* (Fragrant Virgin's Bower) – see page 26.
- *Clematis montana* (Mountain Clematis) – see page 27.
- *Jasminum officinale* (Common White Jasmine) – see page 29.
- *Lonicera japonica* (Japanese Honeysuckle) – see page 29.
- *Lonicera periclymenum* 'Belgica' (Early Dutch Honeysuckle) – see page 30.
- *Lonicera periclymenum* 'Serotina' (Late Dutch Honeysuckle) – see page 30.

Avoid using excessively vigorous climbers

For added interest, occasionally leave peepholes in a trellis

Ensure that the trellis is soundly secured to strong, upright posts

Roses and flowering climbers create feasts of colour – and often with memorable and unusual fragrances – on trellis screens.

Leafy climbers for free-standing screens

The range of leaf-clad climbers for free-standing screens is also wide and includes herbaceous, deciduous and evergreen types. In exposed and windy areas, choose a deciduous or herbaceous type as it will not present such a barrier to strong winter winds. Here are a few climbers to consider.

- *Hedera colchica* 'Dentata Variegata': evergreen – see page 35.
- *Hedera colchica* 'Sulphur Heart': evergreen – see page 35.
- *Humulus lupulus* 'Aureus' (Yellow-leaved Hop): herbaceous – see page 35.
- *Vitis amurensis* (Amurland Grape): deciduous – see page 37.
- *Vitis coignetiae* (Crimson Glory Vine): deciduous – see page 37.
- *Vitis vinifera* 'Purpurea' (Teinturier Grape): deciduous – see page 37.

Roses for free-standing screens

Most free-standing screens are formed of vertical posts with trellis panels 1.8 m (6 ft) long and 1.2–1.5 m (4–5 ft) deep secured between them. Their tops are about 1.8 m (6 ft) high, with a gap between their bases and the ground. Therefore, do not use vigorous climbing roses. Some climbing forms of New English roses are ideal, and these include:

- 'Constance Spry': large, clear-pink, myrrh-scented flowers – see page 42.
- 'Graham Thomas': rich yellow, cup-shaped flowers with a Tea-rose fragrance.
- 'Shropshire Lass': large, semi-double, flesh-pink, fragrant flowers – see page 46.
- 'Snow Goose': large sprays of small, white, pompon-like flowers that have the appearance of large daisies.

Clothing trees and tree stumps

Are tree stumps easy to disguise?

There are several flowering and leafy climbers – as well as roses – that can be used to cloak unsightly tree stumps. These are often the remains of trees that have been cut down, but not to soil level. By clothing them in plants, they can be turned into attractive and unusual features that are sure to capture everyone's attention. Indeed, where there are several unsightly stumps in a group, they can be transformed into an unusual focal point.

Clematis orientalis (Orange-peel Clematis) has fern-like leaves and nodding, star-like, fragrant, yellow flowers, borne from late summer to mid-autumn.

Leafy climbers for clothing tree stumps

Several leafy climbers can be used to cloak low stumps, but first you will need to form a strong tripod – about 1.5 m (5 ft) high – for the plant to straddle.

- *Hedera colchica* 'Sulphur Heart': evergreen – see page 35.
- *Vitis davidii*: deciduous, with coloured leaves in autumn.
- *Vitis riparia*: deciduous, with coloured leaves and sweetly scented flowers.

Clematis for clothing low stumps

Several clematis will clothe a low stump. However, first fix a piece of wire-netting over it so that the clematis has something to cling to.

- *Clematis flammula* – see page 26.
- *Clematis orientalis* – see page 27.
- *Clematis rehderiana* – see page 28.
- *Clematis tangutica* – see page 28.

Roses for clothing tree stumps

Where a tree has been cut down and left as a stump 60 cm (2 ft) high or less, roses can be planted to cloak it and the surrounding ground. Here are a few to consider:

- *Rosa x jacksonii* 'Max Graf': apple-scented, pink flowers.
- 'Rosy Cushion': small, single, pink flowers.
- 'Raubritter': pink flowers, with a sprawling nature and forming a low mound.

Roses for growing into trees

There are several suitable roses; check that the vigour of the rose suits its host.

- 'Bobbie James': Multiflora hybrid with a rambling habit and fragrant, creamy-white flowers – see page 41.
- 'Climbing Cécile Brünner': climber with shell-pink flowers – see page 41.
- 'François Juranville': Wichuraiana-type rambler with coral-pink flowers – see page 43.
- 'Leverkusen': Kordesii-type climber with lemon-yellow flowers – see page 44.
- 'Madame Grégoire Staechelin': climber with coral-pink flowers – see page 44.
- 'Meg': climber with apricot-pink flowers – see page 44.
- 'Paul's Himalayan Musk': rambler with blush to lilac-pink flowers – see page 45.
- 'Veilchenblau': Multiflora-type rambler with dark magenta flowers – see page 47.
- 'Wedding Day': rambler with creamy-white to blush flowers – see page 47.

Clematis

Tropaeolum majus

Roses clothing tree stumps

Cottage-garden climbers

Part of the charm of a cottage garden is its informality and overwhelming aura of peace and tranquillity. Wigwams of Runner Beans and *Lathyrus odoratus* (Sweet Peas), together with cordon- and espalier-trained fruit trees, harmonize with sweetly scented honeysuckles and informal leafy climbers, while herbs and garden flowers clothe the soil around them. Climbers can provide attractive backgrounds, and create height within a large cottage garden.

Is an informal display essential?

Flowering cottage-garden climbers

These have a relaxed appearance, many with richly and unusually fragrant flowers. Here are a few to consider.

- *Clematis armandii*: evergreen, with masses of white, sweetly scented flowers – see page 26.
- *Clematis chrysocoma*: deciduous, with saucer-shaped white flowers – see page 26.
- *Clematis flammula* (Fragrant Virgin's Bower): deciduous, with hawthorn-scented white flowers – see page 26.
- *Fallopia baldshuanica* (Mile-a-minute Vine): deciduous and very vigorous, with masses of pale pink or white flowers – see page 28.
- *Hydrangea anomala* subsp. *petiolaris* (Japanese Climbing Hydrangea): deciduous and vigorous, with creamy-white flowers – see page 29.
- *Jasminum officinale* (Common White Jasmine): deciduous, with fragrant white flowers – see page 29.
- *Lonicera japonica* (Japanese Honeysuckle): evergreen, with sweetly-scented, white to pale yellow flowers – see page 29.
- *Lonicera periclymenum* 'Belgica' (Early Dutch Honeysuckle): deciduous, with sweetly scented purplish-red and yellow flowers – see page 30.
- *Lonicera periclymenum* 'Serotina' (Late Dutch Honeysuckle): deciduous, with sweetly scented flowers, reddish-purple on the outside and creamy-white inside – see page 30.
- *Lonicera tragophylla*: deciduous, with golden-yellow flowers – see page 30.

Leafy climbers for cottage gardens

There are many plants to choose from, some with evergreen foliage, others deciduous. Here is a trio of them.

- *Humulus lupulus* 'Aureus' (Golden-leaved Hop): herbaceous, with yellow leaves and ideal on a tripod or arch – see page 35.
- *Vitis coignetiae* (Crimson Glory Vine): deciduous, with coloured leaves in autumn – see page 37.
- *Vitis vinifera* 'Purpurea' (Dyer's Grape): deciduous, with coloured leaves, especially in autumn – see page 37.

Roses for cottage gardens

Many roses have such a casual and informal nature that they are certain candidates for cottage gardens. Here are a few of them to consider.

- 'Aimée Vibert' – see page 40.
- 'Bobbie James' – see page 41.
- 'François Juranville' – see page 43.
- 'Gerbe Rose' – see page 43.
- 'Madame Grégoire Staechelin' – see page 44.
- 'Noisette Carnée' ('Blush Noisette') – see page 45.
- 'Veilchenblau' – see page 47.
- 'Zéphirine Drouhin' – see page 47.

Annual climbers for cottage gardens

These are ideal for clothing small trellises or wigwams with summer colour. There are many to choose from, including Lathyrus odoratus (Sweet Peas), Ipomoea purpurea (Common Morning Glory), Tropaeolum majus (Nasturtiums) and Tropaeolum peregrinum (Canary Creeper) – see pages 32–33.

Vegetables and fruit trees

Tripods of Runner Beans bring colour and height to a cottage garden – as well as food. Apples and pears, grown as espaliers or cordons, clothe walls or free-standing tiers of supporting wires. See pages 68–69.

Climbers in containers

Surprisingly, a wide range of climbers can be grown in containers, including the herbaceous *Humulus lupulus* 'Aureus' (Yellow-leaved Hop – see far right), clematis (see below) and gloriously coloured annuals (see right), which can be changed each year and include the popular and distinctive *Lathyrus odoratus* (Sweet Pea). Other distinctive flowering plants include wisteria, which needs careful watering and pruning to keep it attractive (see opposite page).

LOOKING AFTER CLIMBERS IN CONTAINERS

Climbers grown in containers need regular attention to ensure that the compost remains moist and does not overheat in summer, when in strong and direct sunlight. Conversely, in winter the compost needs protection from excessive moisture and low temperatures, which might cause the compost to freeze and damage the plants' roots.

In summer, positioning plants in groups helps to shade the pots, but it is not always practical for large climbers. Alternatively, standing the pot on a small paving slab in a border, where it can be surrounded by plants,

helps keep compost cool. Where possible, position the container in light shade.

In winter, covering the compost prevents it becoming saturated; but remove it in late winter. Wrapping the pot in a sandwich created by a polythene (polyethylene) bag loosely filled with straw reduces the risk of freezing.

Annual climbers, such as Ipomoea *(Morning Glory – see top of page 57) create feasts of colour through much of summer. These displays are ideal in small gardens, as they can be changed each year.*

CLEMATIS IN CONTAINERS

Not all clematis are suitable for growing in containers, but here are a few that are worth trying. Always use well-drained, loam-based compost, with plenty of drainage material in the container's base.

- *Clematis armandii:* hardy, evergreen clematis with creamy-white flowers (see page 26). Grow it in a large pot and form a tripod of canes over which it can sprawl. The trailing stems help to keep the compost cool.
- *Clematis florida* 'Sieboldiana:' usually deciduous (sometimes semi-evergreen) shrubby climber with large white flowers with purple centres (see page 26). Choose a sunny but wind-sheltered position – and where the pot is in shade – and support the plant's growth with five or seven canes, 1.2 m (4 ft) long, angled outwards so that stems do not become congested at the climber's centre. Use a large, clay pot, 25–30 cm (10–12 in) in diameter.
- *Clematis macropetala:* moderately vigorous, deciduous and bushy climber with light and dark blue flowers (see page 27). It is magnificent when planted in a tall wooden or terracotta barrel; fill the bottom third of the barrel with coarse drainage material, then well-drained compost. Plant three or five plants at the top and allow the stems to train around the barrel's sides. Stand the barrel on three bricks to ensure that excess moisture can escape from the barrel's base.

- **Large-flowered hybrids:** these are difficult – but not impossible – to grow in large pots, as the compost often overheats. If shading can be provided, these climbers produce a magnificent display, especially 'Marie Boisselot', a deciduous climber with large, pure white flowers (see page 27).

← Clematis florida 'Sieboldiana' *creates an impressive display in a large, decorative pot. The white and purple flowers are distinctive and eye-catching.*

GROWING ANNUALS IN CONTAINERS

Annuals that are raised in gentle warmth in late winter or early spring, and are ready for planting as soon as all risk of frost has passed, are the best ones for growing in containers. Here are a couple of annual climbers to consider.

• *Ipomoea tricolor* **'Heavenly Blue' (Morning Glory):** this annual climber has beautiful sky-blue flowers. You will need to provide it with a trellis about 1.5 m (5 ft) high.

• *Thunbergia alata* **(Black-eyed Susan):** this one has white, orange or yellow flowers with chocolate-brown eyes (see page 33). Provide it with a wigwam of canes.

Sweet Peas in pots and tubs

Lathyrus odoratus (Sweet Pea) is famed for its richly fragrant flowers in a wide colour range, including shades of red, blue, pink and purple. It is a hardy annual, but when grown in a container is best raised as a half-hardy annual. Sow seeds in late winter or early spring in gentle warmth, and pot up plants singly into pots when large enough to handle. Plant into a container when all risk of frost has passed, using three plants in a 25 cm (10 in) wide pot.

Lathyrus odoratus (Sweet Pea)

Stems become drenched in colourful flowers

Fragrant Sweet Peas evoke a cottage-garden atmosphere that can be recreated in pots on patios and in courtyards

Provide a supporting framework of canes or twiggy sticks

Use a large pot, with drainage holes in its base

Yellow-leaved Hop in a tub

Humulus lupulus 'Aureus' (Yellow-leaved Hop) is a hardy herbaceous climber, and once established in a tub can remain there for three or more years, until the compost becomes congested with roots. Each autumn, leaves and stems die down (remove them) and in spring fresh ones appear. In spring, plant three small plants in a tub of well-drained, loam-based compost; form a tripod of five canes to support the plants.

Humulus lupulus 'Aureus' (Yellow-leaved Hop)

Tripod of canes to support the plants

Large pots or tubs of the Yellow-leaved Hop are ideal for positioning on either side of a flight of steps

In spring, the leaves are a rich yellowish-green

Use a large pot or wooden tub

Wisteria in a tub

Wisteria sinensis (Japanese Wisteria) can be planted in a large terracotta pot. Use one 50–60 cm (20–24 in) wide and 30 cm (12 in) deep. The container needs to be wide to create a firm base for the plant. Buy a plant established in a pot and trained with two arms. Alternatively, buy a very young plant and cut it back to about 23 cm (9 in) high. Sideshoots will form; take two and use canes to train them at 45° angles. Both winter and summer pruning are essential.

Wisteria when grown in a large pot instantly attracts attention on a patio or in a courtyard

OTHER CLIMBERS FOR CONTAINERS

• *Clematis* **'Frances Rivis':** violet-blue flowers (see page 26). Form a tripod of canes about 1.5 m (5 ft) high.

• *Jasminum officinale* **(Common White Jasmine):** pure white flowers (see page 29). It needs a warm, wind-sheltered position and supports 1.5–1.8 m (5–6 ft) high.

• *Lapageria rosea* **(Chilean Bell Flower):** rose-crimson flowers (see page 29). A warm, wind-sheltered position is essential, as well as supports 1.5–1.8 m (5–6 ft) high.

Fragrant climbers and wall shrubs

Are there many different scents?

The range of fragrances produced by climbers and wall shrubs includes unusual scents such as cowslip, jasmine and vanilla as well as more familiar ones. There are also plants with sweet-scented flowers; some of these are at their best during evening and early night, when attracting moths to their flowers. The honeysuckles and clematis are especially useful for clothing a romantic arbour or a rustic pergola, when they create a relaxed and informal ambience.

WIDE RANGE OF UNUSUAL FRAGRANCES

Cowslip

- *Clematis rehderiana* (see page 28)
  Delicately and slightly sweet, with a hint of cowslip.

Fruity

- *Magnolia grandiflora* (Bull Bay/Southern Magnolia)
  Fruit-like and sweet; also said to be slightly spicy with a bouquet reminiscent of jasmine or lily-of-the valley, or even of violets and apricots. Evergreen tree or large shrub with creamy-white flowers during mid- and late summer.

Hawthorn

- *Clematis flammula* (see page 26)
  Sweet and resembling hawthorn.

Honey

- *Abeliophyllum distichum* (see page 24) Penetrating, honey-like and sweet.

Jasmine

- *Jasminum officinale* (see page 29) Jasmine-like and sweet.

- *Jasminum polyanthum* (Pink Jasmine)
  Jasmine-like and strongly sweet. Tender, semi-evergreen climber, which is ideal for growing in a greenhouse or conservatory in temperate climates. Tubular, star-shaped, white flowers during late spring and early summer when planted outdoors; or from early winter to spring when in a greenhouse or conservatory. In addition to being grown outdoors, this highly fragrant jasmine is also offered for sale in late winter as a houseplant. When flowering is over, move the plant to a cool greenhouse.

Cytisus battandieri

Pineapple

- *Cytisus battandieri* (see page 28)
  Distinctive pineapple bouquet.

Spicy

- *Chimonanthus praecox* (see page 26)
  Heavy and spicy, with hints of jonquil and violets.

Sweet Pea

- *Lathyrus odoratus* (see page 33)
  Sweet Pea fragrance.

Vanilla

- *Akebia quinata* (see page 24)
  Vanilla-like and sweet; it is also said to be rather spicy and pervasive.

- *Azara microphylla* (see page 25)
  Strongly vanilla-scented.

- *Wisteria floribunda* (see page 31)
  Sweet and vanilla-like.

- *Wisteria sinensis* (see page 31)
  Sweet and vanilla-like.

Wisteria sinensis

SWEET-SCENTED CLIMBERS

Most of the climbers described here are in the A–Z section and on pages 24–31. Others are more fully described. Some of them are also featured on pages 62–65, where advice is given about associating them with other plants.

- *Clematis armandii* (see page 26)
  Sweet.

- *Clematis montana* (see page 27)
  Sweet.

- *Clematis orientalis* (see page 27)
  Slightly sweet.

- *Lonicera × americana*
  Richly sweet. Vigorous, deciduous climber with white flowers that soon change to pale then deep yellow during early and mid-summer.

- *Lonicera caprifolium* (Italian Honeysuckle/Perfoliate Woodbine)
  Richly sweet, especially at night. Vigorous, deciduous climber with creamy-white flowers, tinged pink, during early and mid-summer.

- *Lonicera japonica* (see page 29)
  Sweet.

- *Lonicera periclymenum* 'Belgica' (see page 30)
  Sweet.

- *Lonicera periclymenum* 'Serotina' (see page 30)
  Sweet.

- *Passiflora caerulea* (see page 30)
  Slightly sweet.

USING FRAGRANT CLIMBERS AND WALL SHRUBS

Against walls:
- *Abeliophyllum distichum* – see page 24.
- *Jasminum officinale* – see page 29.
- *Wisteria floribunda* – see page 31.
- *Wisteria sinensis* – see page 31.

For pergolas:
- *Jasmine officinale* – see page 29.
- *Lonicera periclymenum* 'Belgica' – see page 30.
- *Lonicera periclymenum* 'Serotina' – see page 30.
- *Wisteria floribunda* – see page 31.
- *Wisteria sinensis* – see page 31.

On free-standing trellises:
- *Clematis flammula* – see page 26.
- *Clematis montana* – see page 27.
- *Lonicera japonica* – see page 29.
- *Lonicera periclymenum* 'Belgica' – see page 30.
- *Lonicera periclymenum* 'Serotina' – see page 30.

Scented annuals on low arches:
- *Lathyrus odoratus* – see page 33.
- *Tropaeolum majus* (slightly fragrant) – see page 33.

SCENTED GARDENS FOR THE VISUALLY CHALLENGED

- **Suitable climbers:** check that the chosen climber does not have prickly stems or ones that will block paths under arches, or become free and whip around in strong winds.
- **Positioning:** do not position paths close to trellises or the sides of arches. Use gravel to indicate the width of the path; a path formed of paving slabs positioned along the centre and surrounded on each side by 30 cm (1 ft) wide strips of gravel gives a sound warning of its position.
- **Arches and pergolas:** check that the height and width enable easy and safe access.

Fragrant arbours

Many superbly scented flowering climbers can be used to cloak arbours. Some, such as honeysuckles and several clematis, create an informal and cottage-garden feel, while wisteria has a more formal stance when grown on a clinically shaped arbour.

- *Clematis flammula* (Fragrant Virgin's Bower) – see page 26.
- *Clematis montana* (Mountain Clematis) – see page 27.
- *Jasminum officinale* (Common White Jasmine) – see page 29.
- *Lonicera periclymenum* 'Belgica' (Early Dutch Honeysuckle) – see page 30.
- *Lonicera periclymenum* 'Serotina' (Late Dutch Honeysuckle) – see page 30.
- *Wisteria floribunda* (Japanese Wisteria) – see page 31.
- *Wisteria sinensis* (Chinese Wisteria) – see page 31.

Cloistered arbours, drenched in heady fragrances, create memorable features, especially in small gardens.

Fragrant climbing and rambling roses

Are there unusual fragrances?

Many climbing and rambling roses have exciting and unexpected fragrances, and several of them are featured here. Fragrances range from apple, through myrrh, to the distinctive bouquet of a Tea rose, which is defined as the smell emitted by a freshly opened packet of tea and said to be slightly tarry. Many of the roses suggested here are detailed in the **A–Z** section of roses (see pages 40–47). The others are described more fully on these pages.

AMAZING FRAGRANCES

The fragrances created by climbing and rambling roses will amaze you with their variety and range. Here are some that will tempt you to plant them.

Apple

- 'Alexandre Girault' (see page 41) – richly apple-like.
- 'Auguste Gervais' – richly apple-like. Wichuraiana-type rambler with semi-double, coppery-yellow and salmon flowers. Up to 6 m (20 ft) high.
- 'François Juranville' (see page 43) – sharp and apple-like.
- 'La Perle' – fresh green apples and lemon. Wichuraiana-type rambler with fully double, quartered, creamy-white flowers. Up to 7.5 m (25 ft) high.
- 'Paul Transon' (see page 45) – strongly apple-like.
- 'René André' – sweet and apple-like. Wichuraiana-type rambler with small, slightly cupped, soft apricot-yellow flowers flushed pink. It grows 5.4–6 m (18–20 ft) high.

Clove

- 'Noisette Carnée' (see page 45) – rich and clove-like.

Fruity

- 'Albéric Barbier' (see page 40) – fresh and fruity.
- 'New Dawn' (see page 45) – fruity fragrance.

Lemon

- 'Leverkusen' (see page 44) – distinctive lemon fragrance.

Musk

- 'Aimée Vibert' (see page 40) – distinct and musk-like.

Myrrh

- 'Constance Spry' (see page 42) – strongly myrrh-like.
- 'Shropshire Lass' (see page 46) – myrrh-like.
- 'St Swithun' (see page 46) – strongly myrrh-like.

Orange

- 'The Garland' (see page 46) – rich orange-like fragrance.
- 'Veilchenblau' (see page 47) – rich orange-like fragrance.
- 'Wedding Day' (see page 47) – sweet, with a hint of orange.

Orange and banana

- 'Francis E. Lester' – richly sweet fusion of orange and banana. Rambler, with clusters of small, single blush to white flowers. It grows 3.6–4.5 m (12–15 ft) high.

Paeony

- 'Gerbe Rose' (see page 43) – delicious paeony-like fragrance.

Primrose

- 'Adélaïde d'Orléans' (see page 40) – delicate primrose fragrance.
- 'Félicité Perpétue' – delicate primrose fragrance. Sempervirens-type rambler, with large clusters of small, creamy-white flowers. It grows 4.5–6 m (15–20 ft) high.

Raspberry

- 'Zéphirine Drouhin' (see page 47) – sweet and penetrating, with a slight raspberry-like bouquet.

AMAZING FRAGRANCES (CONTINUED)

Sweet Pea

- 'Madame Grégoire Staechelin' (see page 44) – delicious Sweet Pea fragrance.

Tea-rose fragrance

- 'Alister Stella Gray' (see page 41) – strongly sweet and Tea-rose fragrance.

- 'Climbing Lady Hillingdon' (see page 42) – delicious Tea-rose fragrance.

- 'Climbing Souvenir de la Malmaison' – delicious Tea-rose fragrance. Bourbon-type climber, with globular, blush-pink flowers. It grows about 3.6 m (12 ft) high.

- 'Graham Thomas' (see page 47) – Tea-rose fragrance and yellow flowers.

SWEETLY SCENTED CLIMBERS AND RAMBLERS

Rosa 'Sander's White Rambler'

- 'Albertine' (see page 41) – rich and sweet.

- 'Gloire de Dijon' (see page 43) – sweet and penetrating.

- 'Golden Showers' (see page 43) – pleasingly sweet.

- 'Guinée' (see page 43) – richly sweet.

- 'Kathleen Harrop' (see page 44) – very sweet.

- 'Madame Alfred Carrière' (see page 44) – sweet and strong.

- 'Maigold' (see page 44) – sweet and strong.

- 'Mermaid' (see page 45) – sweet and delicate.

- 'Rambling Rector' (see page 46) – deliciously sweet.

- 'Sander's White Rambler' (see page 46) – deliciously sweet and fresh.

USING SCENTED ROSES

Against walls:
- 'Adélaïde d'Orléans' – see page 40.
- 'Aimée Vibert' – see page 40.
- 'Climbing Lady Hillingdon' – see page 42.
- 'François Juranville – see page 43.

For pergolas:
- 'Albéric Barbier' – see page 40.
- 'Albertine' – see page 41.
- 'François Juranville' – see page 43.
- 'Veilchenblau' – see page 47.

On pillars and tripods:
- 'Golden Showers' – see page 43.
- 'Leverkusen' – see page 44.
- 'Maigold' – see page 44.

On arches:
- 'Albéric Barbier' – see page 40.
- 'Albertine' – see page 41.
- 'François Juranville' – see page 43.
- 'Veilchenblau' – see page 47.

ROSE-COVERED GAZEBOS

With a long heritage and a name meaning 'to gaze out', gazebos are distinctive garden features, especially when positioned to have a wide vantage point. Fragrant climbers are often used to partly clothe them, but roses with their distinguished history are also worth considering. Ramblers, with their relaxed habit and massed flowers, are ideal for clambering over gazebos.

MAKING YOUR OWN GAZEBO

Constructing your own gazebo needs careful planning if it is to merge with the rest of the garden and not look like a tatty bandstand or neglected bus stop. Whatever the design that appeals to you may be, the construction must be sound, including foundations for posts. If its construction is beyond your skills, sketch the style you like and ask a local carpenter or builder to give you a quote (estimate) for the work.

Plant associations with climbers and wall shrubs

Are good combinations hard to achieve?

To create a more spectacular display than when shrubs and wall shrubs are grown on their own, other plants can be added to form handsome combinations. This is not difficult, and pleasing medleys of flowers as well as attractive foliage can be easily achieved. This also helps to extend the season of interest. On this and the following pages, exciting and usually inexpensive combinations of climbers and wall shrubs are suggested.

COLOUR WHEELS

The simplest wheel is formed of six colours – red, violet, blue, green, yellow and orange. Colours that are opposite each other are complementary, while those in adjacent segments create harmonizing combinations.

MIXING AND MATCHING CLIMBERS AND WALL SHRUBS

The range of combinations for climbers and wall shrubs is wide and involves many different plants. Here are a few to try.

Involving large-flowered clematis

• Plant *Clematis* 'Lasurstern', with rich, deep blue flowers with conspicuous creamy-white stamens during early summer and later in late summer and into early autumn, with *Lonicera* x *tellmanniana*. This honeysuckle bears whorls of red-and-yellow flowers during early and mid-summer. It needs a sunny wall.

• For a duo of large-flowered clematis, try 'Perle d'Azur' (light blue with a pinkish-mauve flush) and 'Ville de Lyon' (bright carmine-red with golden stamens).

• Where a wisteria is planted against a wall, plant *Clematis* 'Lasurstern' close by so that its rich-blue flowers are able to associate with the fragrant, mauve flowers of the wisteria.

SIZE AND SHAPE CONTRAST

Positioning flowers with shape and size contrasts close to each other soon captures the eye. Here, the bright blue Clematis *'Perle d'Azur' and* Bupleurum fruticosa, *with its sea-green foliage and yellow flowers, form a striking combination.*

↗ Clematis *'Ville de Lyon' has large, bright carmine-red flowers with a reddish tinge around the edges. It forms an exciting and memorable colour combination with* Lonicera japonica *(Japanese Honeysuckle).*

↗ *The Floribunda rose 'Elizabeth of Glamis' has salmon-pink flowers. They create a memorable display when planted with* Clematis *'Huldine', which bears pearly-white and pale mauve flowers.*

↗ *Use a strongly coloured* Clematis, *perhaps in a strong deep mauve, and plant it amid a colour-leaved form of* Cornus alba *'Spaethii' (Red-barked Dogwood), which is deciduous, with variegated leaves.*

MIXING AND MATCHING CLIMBERS AND WALL SHRUBS (CONTINUED)

Using species clematis

- Plant the hardy, deciduous climber *Clematis chrysocoma*, with white flowers during early and mid-summer, next to a dark red or pink form of *Chaenomeles speciosa* (Japanese Quince), a deciduous, spring-flowering shrub.
- For a combination of a large-leaved climber and a yellow-flowered clematis, plant *Clematis tangutica* in front of the vigorous *Vitis coignetiae* (Crimson Glory Vine). In autumn, the rounded, but lobed, mid-green leaves of this leafy climber assume rich colours that contrast with the rich yellow, late summer to mid-autumn flowers of the clematis.
- For a spring display, plant *Clematis* 'Frances Rivis' on the shaded side of a wall, about 1.2–1.5 m (4–5 ft) high, and allow the stems to trail over it and on to the sunny side. By planting the deciduous shrub *Kerria japonica* 'Pleniflora' on the sunny side the violet-blue, mid- and late spring flowers of the clematis will harmonize with the orange-yellow flowers of the *Kerria*, often known as Bachelor's Buttons.

Involving Winter-flowering Jasmine

- Plant the evergreen shrub *Mahonia aquifolium* in front of *Jasminum nudiflorum* (Winter-flowering Jasmine). The yellow flowers of the jasmine contrast with the holly-like leaves of the Mahonia, which turn bronze-red in winter.
- Plant a *Jasminum nudiflorum* (Winter-flowering Jasmine) against a winter-shaded wall, with pink forms of *Erica carnea* (Winter-flowering Heather) in front. The variety 'Springwood Pink', with rich pink flowers, is a good choice.
- Plant *Jasminum nudiflorum* (Winter-flowering Jasmine) against a cool wall, with a *Camellia sasanqua* in front of it. The pink flowers of the camellia complement the yellow-flowered jasmine.
- For a combination of *Jasminum nudiflorum* (Winter-flowering Jasmine) and *Cotoneaster horizontalis*, see page 64. In addition to clothing a wall, it is ideal for planting at the base of an informal, flint-faced, 1.4–1.5 m (4–5 ft) high wall, where it can be encouraged to spread over the top.

↗ Clematis x durandii *is a superb hybrid, with dark blue flowers with central clusters of yellow stamens throughout much of summer. It combines well with the fragrant, single, white flowers of* Rosa multiflora.

↗ *The large-flowered* Clematis *'Duchess of Edinburgh', with large, double, fragrant, white flowers with green shading in early summer, combines well with the purple-blue of* Solanum crispum *'Glasnevin'.*

Clematis harmonies

As well as creating strongly coloured contrasts, clematis can be used to produce attractive harmonies. Here, three different combinations are illustrated.

The climbing rose 'Zéphirine Drouhin' has masses of fragrant, deep rose-pink flowers and forms a magnificent display when combined with the rich-red flowers of the large-flowered hybrid Clematis 'Niobe'.

Clematis 'Madame Julia Correvon', with rosy-red flowers about 13 cm (5 in) wide, creates a handsome duo when planted with the rambling rose 'American Pillar': it has single, bright pink flowers.

Clematis viticella has violet, reddish-purple or blue flowers during mid-summer and into early autumn. They harmonize with the Berberis x ottawensis, a deciduous shrub with rounded or oval green leaves.

MIXING AND MATCHING CLIMBERS AND WALL SHRUBS (CONTINUED)

Scented wall-shrub combination

- Plant the mid- to late-winter-flowering *Chimonanthus praecox* (Wintersweet), with its spicy-scented flowers and yellow petals and purple centres, close to *Lonicera fragrantissima*, which is a partially evergreen shrub with strongly fragrant, creamy-white flowers from mid-winter to early spring.

Autumn-coloured combinations

- For a duo of autumn colour, plant the deciduous shrub *Berberis thunbergii* in front of *Parthenocissus henryana* (Chinese Virginia Creeper). In autumn, the leaves of the *Berberis* turn brilliant red and complement the leaves of the Chinese Virginia Creeper.
- Plant *Vitis coignetiae* (Crimson Glory Vine) to clamber into a white-stemmed birch, which acts as a superb colour contrast for the rounded, but lobed, mid-green leaves which, in autumn, assume rich colours.

Involving honeysuckles

- *Lonicera periclymenum* 'Belgica (Early Dutch Honeysuckle), with its sweetly scented, purplish-red and yellow flowers during late spring and early summer, is a perfect partner for rambler-type rose 'Albertine'. It has fragrant, light salmon-pink flowers. An alternative rose to combine with the honeysuckle is *Rosa bracteata* (Macartney Rose), which has large, single, silky-white flowers up to 10 cm (4 in) across. The Macartney Rose, native to eastern China, is best planted against a warm, wind-sheltered wall.

Annual climber combinations

- The annual *Lathyrus odoratus* (Sweet Pea) is easily grown and when given pea-sticks or bamboo canes as supports and positioned behind the dense, clump-forming *Salvia* x *superba*, with slender spires of purple flowers, creates a superb feature. Choose a deep pink-flowered variety of Sweet Pea.

Involving ivies

- On a wall or free-standing trellis, mixing several variegated ivies creates an attractive feature. A duo of *Hedera colchica* 'Sulphur Heart', with deep green leaves splashed and irregularly streaked bright yellow, and *Hedera colchica* 'Dentata Variegata', with bright green leaves with pale green and creamy-white edges, is attractive. However, 'Sulphur Heart' is more vigorous than 'Dentata Variegata' and, unless regularly cut back, will eventually dominate its companion.
- On a wall, a combination of *Hedera canariensis* 'Gloire de Marengo' (Variegated Canary Island Ivy) forms an attractive partnership with the small-leaved *Hedera helix* 'Buttercup'. The Variegated Canary Island Ivy has deep green leaves with edges merging into silvery-grey and white, while those of 'Buttercup' are rich yellow, becoming yellowish-green or pale green with age.
- Plant the large-flowered *Clematis* 'Ernest Markham', with bright magenta flowers, to partially cloak a wall with *Hedera helix* 'Goldheart', with shiny green leaves that display yellow splashes at their centres. In some nurseries you will see this ivy listed as *Hedera helix* 'Oro di Bogliasco'.

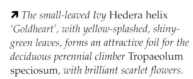

↗ Jasminum nudiflorum *(Winter-flowering Jasmine), with bright yellow flowers from late autumn to late spring, looks superb when peering through the stems of Cotoneaster horizontalis.*

↗ *The small-leaved Ivy* Hedera helix *'Goldheart', with yellow-splashed, shiny-green leaves, forms an attractive foil for the deciduous perennial climber* Tropaeolum speciosum, *with brilliant scarlet flowers.*

↗ *The deciduous* Actinidia kolomikta *(Kolomikta Vine), with pink or white ends to its leaves, forms an exciting combination with* Eccremocarpus scaber *and* Lonicera japonica *'Halliana'.*

BACKGROUND COLOURS FOR CLIMBERS AND WALL SHRUBS

In addition to selecting climbers and wall shrubs that form handsome combinations with other plants, it is also possible to create spectacular displays by positioning them against coloured walls. Here are a few climbers and wall shrubs for you to consider.

Red-brick walls

Choose plants with white, soft blue, silver or lemon flowers, such as:

- Abeliophyllum distichum (page 24): white
- Carpenteria californica (page 25): white
- Ceanothus thyrsiflorus var. repens (page 25): light blue
- Clematis armandii (page 26): creamy-white
- Clematis chrysocoma (page 26): white
- Clematis 'Marie Boisselot' (page 27): white
- Clematis rehderiana (page 28): soft primrose-yellow
- Hydrangea anomala subsp. petiolaris (page 29): creamy-white
- Jasminum officinale (page 29): pure white
- Lonicera japonica (page 29) : white to pale yellow
- Solanum laxum (page 30): pale blue
- Trachelospermum jasminoides (page 31): white
- Wisteria sinensis (page 31): mauve

Grey-stone walls

Choose plants with deep purple, pink, deep blue or red flowers, such as:

- Berberidopsis corallina (page 25): deep red
- Ceanothus cuneatus var. rigidus (page 25): purple-blue
- Clematis 'Frances Rivis' (page 26): violet-blue
- Clematis 'Ville de Lyon' (page 28): carmine-red
- Lapageria rosea (page 29): rose-crimson
- Solanum crispum (page 30): purple-blue
- Wisteria floribunda (page 31): violet-blue

White walls

Choose plants with yellow, gold, or scarlet flowers, such as:

- Abutilon megapotamicum (page 24): scarlet and yellow
- Azara microphylla (page 25): yellow
- Chimonanthus praecox (page 26): yellow, with purple centres
- Clematis orientalis (page 27): yellow
- Clematis tangutica (page 28): rich yellow
- Cytisus battandieri (page 28): golden-yellow
- Fremontodendron californicum (page 28): golden-yellow
- Jasminum nudiflorum (page 29): bright yellow
- Lonicera periclymenum 'Belgica' (page 30): purplish-red and yellow
- Lonicera tragophylla (page 30): golden-yellow

↗ The small-leaved Ivy Hedera helix 'Buttercup', with rich yellow leaves, when young, creates an attractive duo with the semi-double, deepish pink flowers of the lightly scented climbing rose 'Bantry Bay'.

↗ Jasminum officinale (Common White Jasmine) forms an attractive partnership with the light and dark blue flowers of Clematis macropetala and deep purple-blue flowers of Lavandula 'Hidcote'. This lavender is ideal for planting around the base of the display, as it grows only 45–60 cm (18–24 in) high. The foliage is also attractive. This lavender flowers from mid-summer to early autumn.

Plant associations with roses

Why use roses?

Using roses to create spectacular and long-term features is becoming increasingly popular, especially in small gardens where space is limited. For example, trellis-like porches over front doors can become awash with colour from a climbing rose on one side and another climber on the other. Scented and colour harmonizing plants can be planted around the rose's base. This and other attractive combinations are illustrated and described on these pages.

INSPIRATIONAL ASSOCIATIONS WITH ROSES

In addition to the many illustrated and described plants associated with climbing and rambling roses suggested on pages 62–65, here are others to consider.

- *Rosa banksiae* 'Lutea', a rambler with small, double, cupped, deep-yellow flowers that hang in sprays in late spring and early summer, forms an attractive association with a mauve wisteria. Both can be trained on a wall or pergola.
- The rambler 'Bobbie James' is a Multiflora type, with a mass of small, creamy-white, semi-double flowers. It is a vigorous rose, ideal for covering pergolas, growing into trees and covering unsightly features. The creamy-white flowers harmonize with blue flowers; therefore plant the lavender-blue-flowered *Nepeta* x *faassenii* (Catmint) around its base. It remains in flower from late spring to early autumn.
- The Modern climber 'New Dawn', with silvery blush-pink flowers, grows about 3 m (10 ft) high and forms an attractive combination with *Clematis* 'Perle d'Azure'. The Clematis, with its light blue flowers with a pinkish-mauve flush, will sprawl and clamber among the rose stems.
- The New English rose 'Constance Spry' has both a shrubby and a climbing habit. Its clear rose-pink flowers form an attractive combination with silver-leaved plants that have been positioned around it.
- The Modern climber 'Aloha' is a low-growing climber, often with a short and bushy habit. It has large, cupped, fragrant, pink flowers that harmonize with light blue-flowered plants positioned around its base. It can also be combined with *Lonicera periclymenum* 'Belgica' (Early Dutch Honeysuckle).
- The climber 'Guinée' has large, double, very dark flowers, borne mainly during early summer but often making a repeat flowering. They combine well with honeysuckle or *Clematis viticella*, which bears large, nodding, violet, reddish-purple of blue flowers during mid- and late summer, and sometimes into early autumn.

↖ *The large-flowered hybrid* Clematis *'Jackmanii Superba' has large, rich violet-purple flowers with a reddish tinge and golden stamens. They create an attractive combination with the silvery, blush-pink flowers of the rose 'New Dawn', a Modern climber.*

↗ Clematis montana *(Mountain Clematis), with white flowers, and the rose 'Helen Knight' form an attractive combination. The clear yellow flowers of the rose contrast with those of the clematis.*

BACKGROUND COLOURS FOR ROSES

In the same way that climbers and wall shrubs can be colour-coordinated with walls (see page 65), so too can roses. If the rose is more suited for growing up a formal pergola with square-edged and planed timber, paint the framework to suit the rose's colour. Here are a few combinations to consider.

Red-brick walls

Choose roses with white, soft blue, silver or lemon flowers, such as:

- 'Aimée Vibert' (page 40): pure white
- 'Albéric Barbier' (page 40): creamy-white
- 'Bobbie James' (page 41): creamy-white
- 'Gloire de Dijon' (page 43): buff-yellow
- 'Leverkusen' (page 44): lemon-yellow
- 'Rêve d'Or' (page 46): buff-yellow with pink shading
- 'Sander's White Rambler' (page 46): white
- 'Wedding Day' (page 47): creamy-white to blush

Grey-stone walls

Choose roses with deep purple, pink, deep blue or red flowers, such as:

- 'Adélaïde d'Orléans' (page 40): creamy-pink
- 'Aloha' (page 41): pink
- 'Climbing Cécile Brünner' (page 41): shell-pink
- 'Climbing Lady Sylvia' (page 42): pale pink, with a yellow base
- 'Constance Spry' (page 42): clear rose-pink
- 'Gerbe Rose' (page 43): pink
- 'Kathleen Harrop' (page 44): light pink
- 'Meg' (page 44): apricot-pink
- 'New Dawn' (page 45): silvery blue-pink
- 'Noisette Carnée' (page 45): lilac-pink
- 'Pink Perpétué' (page 45): pink flowers with carmine reverses
- 'Shropshire Lass' (page 46): delicate pink, fading to white
- 'Zéphirine Drouhin' (page 47): deep rose-pink

White walls

Choose roses with yellow, gold or scarlet flowers, such as:

- 'Climbing Crimson Glory' (page 42): deep crimson
- 'Climbing Lady Hillingdon' (page 42): apricot-yellow
- 'Crimson Shower' (page 42): bright crimson
- 'Danse du Feu' (page 43): brilliant orange-scarlet
- 'Golden Showers' (page 43): bright yellow
- 'Guinée' (page 43): dark red
- 'Mermaid' (page 45): primrose-yellow

↗ *The rambling rose 'Albéric Barbier' has yellow buds that open to reveal large, double, creamy-white flowers with a fruit fragrance. It harmonizes well with* Euphorbia characias, *a herbaceous perennial with dark blue-grey leaves that remain evergreen in mild areas. Sulphur-yellow flowers appear during late spring and early summer.* ↗ *Sweet Peas, with their distinctive fragrances and wide range of colours, harmonize with many shrub roses.*

Climbing and scrambling vegetables

Are there many climbing vegetables?

Runner Beans (also known as **Scarlet Runners**) are the most popular climbing vegetables, and when first introduced into Europe were grown solely for their attractive flowers. The plant is still a popular food climber for cottage and other types of gardens, providing food as well as being decorative and creating a dense screen of leaves, scarlet flowers and edible beans. Garden Peas are another vegetable with a climbing or sprawling habit.

USING RUNNER BEANS IN GARDENS

This is a versatile vegetable, which is sown fresh each year, as soon as all risk of frost has passed. Plants can be supported in several ways.

- Bean poles are the traditional method of supporting plants, with two rows of poles, 45 cm (1½ ft) apart, inward-facing and 30 cm (1 ft) apart in the rows. Long poles across the top hold the vertical poles in position. These are ideal for creating a peep-proof screen across a garden.
- Wigwams, formed of 3–5 poles, create ideal supports where only a few plants are to be grown. They are also superb for introducing height to cottage gardens and other informal areas, where they create brightly coloured focal points when in flower.
- Nets, with a 5 cm (2 in) mesh and supported and strained by wires between posts, create a screen. They need to be about 1.8 m (6 ft) high – and well supported to prevent damage from summer storms.

Runner Beans are ideal for screening a vegetable plot from the rest of the garden as well as being productive.

Sowing seeds and raising plants

The easiest and most inexpensive way to grow Runner Beans is to sow seeds in the positions where they will germinate and grow.

- In late spring (in mild areas) or early summer (for cold regions) sow seeds 5 cm (2 in) deep and about 7.5 cm (3 in) from the base of each pole. Keep the soil moist but not waterlogged. Germination takes about two weeks.

- Alternatively, buy established plants and plant them as soon as all risk of frost has passed.

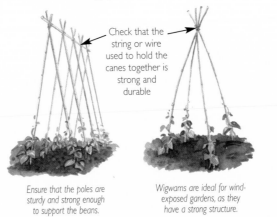

Check that the string or wire used to hold the canes together is strong and durable

Ensure that the poles are sturdy and strong enough to support the beans.

Wigwams are ideal for wind-exposed gardens, as they have a strong structure.

GARDEN PEAS

These have both a sprawling and climbing habit: use either twiggy sticks pushed into the soil for dwarf types, especially early-maturing varieties, or wire-netting about 1.2 m (4 ft) high and supported by stout bamboo canes or posts.

Wall-trained fruit

Several popular tree fruits (such as apples and pears) can be grown against a wall, where they make the best use of space in a small garden as well as benefiting from a wind-sheltered position. Peaches – and their smooth-skinned relatives, the popular nectarines – especially benefit from a sunny wall when grown in temperate climates. However, raspberries, blackberries and hybrid berries (see below) need a more open situation, but are also supported by wires.

Can I grow fruit against a wall?

TREE FRUITS

The tree fruits most popular with home gardeners for growing against walls or alongside paths are:
- **Apples:** use dwarfing rootstocks such as M27 and M9, and choose a space-saving form (see below). Also choose varieties not readily available in shops.
- **Pears:** use the Quince A rootstock, and train trees as espaliers or cordons. Pears need pollination partners, so grow three different varieties as cordons, such as 'Conference', 'Doyenné du Comice' and 'Williams' Bon Chrétien'.
- **Peaches and nectarines:** use St Julien A rootstock, and grow as a fan.

SPACE-SAVING FRUIT TREE SHAPES (SUPPORTING WIRES ARE NEEDED)

- **Cordons:** single-stemmed trees, usually grown at an angle of about 45°. Ideal for apples and pears.
- **Espalier:** lateral branches on two sides are trained in equally spaced tiers. Ideal for apples and pears.
- **Fan-trained:** distinctive and ideal for planting against a wall. Not widely used for apples and pears, more popular with peaches and nectarines.

Warm, wind-sheltered walls are especially useful for growing peaches and nectarines. Support them with tiered wires.

More climbing fruits

Several soft fruits are grown supported by a framework of tiered wires and, perhaps, alongside a path or in a fruit garden.

- **Raspberries:** need a supporting framework of tiered wires, 30–38 cm (12–15 in) apart to 1.6 m (5½ ft) high. These are strained between strong posts, 1.8 m (6 ft) high and in full sun. Space plants 45 cm (1½ ft) apart. There are both 'summer' and 'autumn' fruiting types (do not mix them).

- **Blackberries:** create a supporting framework of wires, 90 cm (3 ft), 1.2 m (4 ft), 1.5 m (5 ft) and 1.8 m (6 ft) high. Space plants 1.8–3.6 m (6–12 ft) apart, depending on the variety's vigour.

- **Hybrid berries:** Grow and space plants in the same way as for blackberries (see above).

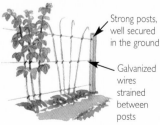

Fertile, moisture-retentive soil is essential for cane fruits

Strong posts, well secured in the ground

Galvanized wires strained between posts

GROWING A FIG

This slightly tender fruit, native to an area from Syria to Afghanistan, is deciduous and not fully hardy in cold, temperate regions. Therefore, choose a wind-sheltered, sunny wall. Unless the roots of figs are restricted in a 60 cm (2 ft) square hole, perhaps lined on four sides with 60 cm (2 ft) square paving slabs, plants become rampant. Fill the base of the hole with 23 cm (9 in) of clean brick rubble, then top up with a mixture of soil-based compost and a dusting of bonemeal. Plant your fig in early spring. A supporting framework of tiered wires, at 30 cm (1 ft) intervals from 30 cm (1 ft) to 3 m (10 ft) high, is essential. Space plants about 3.6 m (12 ft) apart.

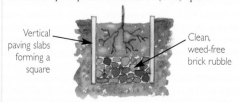

Vertical paving slabs forming a square

Clean, weed-free brick rubble

Formal garden displays

Are formal climbers possible?

Many gardens, especially those on high-density new housing developments, are formal and rectangular. They therefore need plants, including climbers and wall shrubs, that maintain this theme. No climbers have strictly clinical outlines, but those with a non-rampant nature are the best for this situation. Several wall shrubs have a neat habit. Part of this formality is exemplified by the supporting structure – use clinically planed wood rather than rustic poles.

FORMAL WALL SHRUBS

Several formal wall shrubs are diminutive enough for small gardens, where they create colour for most of the year. Here are a few to consider.

Summer flowers
• *Abutilon megapotamicum*: evergreen, with scarlet and yellow flowers from late spring to early autumn (see page 24).
• *Carpenteria californica*: evergreen, with white, fragrant flowers during early and mid-summer (see page 25).
• *Ceanothus thyrsiflorus* var. *repens*: evergreen, with blue flowers during late spring and early summer (see page 25).

Autumn and winter colour
• *Pyracantha rogersiana* 'Flava': evergreen, with bright yellow fruits in autumn and winter (see page 39).
• *Pyracantha* 'Orange Glow': evergreen, with bright orange-red fruits which appear in autumn and last well into winter.
• *Pyracantha coccinea* 'Lalandei': evergreen, with orange-red fruits densely covering branches in autumn and winter.

↖ Several Pyracantha spp. (Firethorns) can be pruned and trained in a formal manner to clothe walls beneath and around windows. They are especially useful for planting against cold walls, surviving in positions where many climbers would fail.

FORMAL CLIMBERS

Climbers have a more relaxed appearance than wall shrubs and therefore fewer are candidates for formal gardens. However, formal pergolas – perhaps constructed of planed and painted timber (beams) – help in the quest for formality. Wisteria, with its lax and pendulous clusters of mauve or white flowers, has a 'dual personality' and can be used in both informal and formal ways. Few eyes are not captured by a white-flowered form trailing flowers over an old brick wall, while when cascading from a formal pergola it creates a different feel altogether. By painting the framework battleship-grey, the flowers are further enhanced and given formality.

→ As well as bearing distinctive flowers, in autumn the leaves assume rich colours. These are usually at their best when this wisteria is grown against a wall.

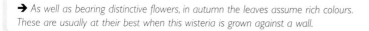

USING ROSES FORMALLY

↗ 'Violette' is a Multiflora rose, with clusters of small, double, lightly scented, crimson-purple flowers with golden stamens. Usually, the flowers fade to an attractive maroon that harmonizes with the dark foliage. It has a rambling habit but is sufficiently diminutive, up to 3.6 m (12 ft), for clothing a metal arch in a small garden.

Apart from clothing walls, roses can be used in other ways in formal gardens, including dressing pergolas and covering pillars and tripods. Mainly, it is small- and single-flowered roses that create the impression of formality; large-flowered varieties are more informal, especially when their flowers are fully open and exposed to wet and blustery winds. Under these conditions, small-flowered varieties have a better chance of retaining formality.

Against walls

- 'Climbing Pompon de Paris': a climbing miniature rose with twiggy growth and masses of rose-pink, pompon-like flowers in early summer. It is not repeat-flowering, but is ideal for planting between a wall and a path where, perhaps, only 30 cm (1 ft) of space and soil exists. It has greyish-green foliage and grows only 2.1 m (7 ft) high.
- 'Helen Knight': you might see this beautiful rose listed as Rosa ecae 'Helen Knight'. It has single, clear yellow, faintly fragrant, 3.5 cm (1½ in) wide flowers during early

summer, amid dainty, fern-like foliage. It grows about 2.1 m (7 ft) high and wide; unfortunately, it is not repeat-flowering, but the foliage creates an attractive background for other plants.

Clothing pergolas

- 'American Pillar': although an old variety and to many rose authorities now superseded by new varieties, this rambler has single, deep pink flowers with a white eye in the latter parts of early summer and into mid-summer.
- 'Crimson Shower': a rambler with a free-flowering nature and displaying large clusters of crimson flowers during mid-summer and into early autumn.

↗ Rosa 'Crimson Shower'

Dressing pillars

- 'Dortmund': a beautiful repeat-flowering climber with single, red flowers with a white eye, initially produced in early summer. Remember to cut out dead flowers to extend the flowering season.
- 'Parkdirektor Riggers': a hardy repeat-flowering rose with semi-double, blood-red flowers, initially produced in early summer. Remove dead flowers.

← Pillar roses create dramatic features, either on their own or in a line and perhaps following the curve of a path. Position the pillars with 1.8–2.4 m (6–8 ft) between them, so that surrounding grass can be easily cut. This also ensures that there is a good circulation of air around the roses.

Climbers as hedges

Afew climbers can be encouraged to form informal hedges, either on their own or by sprawling over low wrought-iron fencing or meandering through an established hedge, for example. These hedges are informal and are ideal in rural areas as well as in towns, where fences need to be clothed to produce a more attractive appearance. Some climbers, especially when they are bearing colourful flowers, are also good for covering the tops of low walls.

Rosa 'Zéphirine Drouhin' is a climber that also can be planted to form a hedge with a wealth of colourful flowers.

CLIMBERS AS HEDGES

Lonicera japonica (Japanese Honeysuckle) can be planted so that it clambers through wrought-iron railings to resemble a hedge.

> ### Two climbing roses as hedges
>
> A few climbing roses create unusual and spectacular hedges, including:
>
> • **'Shropshire Lass':** New English Rose that can be grown as a bush or as a climber. It bears large, semi-double, flesh-pink flowers fading to white. Forms a hedge 1.2–1.8 m (4–6 ft) high.
>
> • **'Zéphirine Drouhin':** Bourbon climber with fragrant, deep rose-pink flowers. Forms a hedge 1.8–2.4 m (6–8 ft) high.

Two climbers are often used to create hedges, where they produce magnificent displays of flowers. These are:
• *Lonicera japonica* (**Japanese Honeysuckle**): a slow-growing, evergreen climber, often scaling 4.5 m (15 ft) or more. Yet, when planted to clothe a fence about 90 cm (3 ft) high, it produces a dense covering of leaves and fragrant, white to pale yellow flowers from early summer to autumn.
• *Clematis montana* (**Mountain Clematis**): a vigorous, deciduous climber that will easily clothe a large trellis, when it produces pure white flowers in late spring and early summer. It can also be allowed to clamber over an existing, perhaps unexciting hedge or, better, over a palisade of stakes that provide firm support.

LEAFY CLIMBERS OVER LOW WALLS

If you have an unsightly low wall, or an old picket fence that is still strong but not very attractive, smothering it with the leaves of the hardy, deciduous climber *Vitis vinifera* 'Purpurea' (Dyer's Grape) will give it renewed vitality. The large, rounded, claret-coloured leaves assume rich purple shades in autumn, before falling. As a bonus it has dark, purple fruits.

The wine-dark leaves of Vitis vinifera *'Purpurea' contrast superbly with a white picket fence.*

RUSTIC HEDGES

Climbers can be introduced into rural hedges, perhaps formed of a medley of plants including *Crataegus* (Hawthorn), *Viburnum lantana* (Wayfaring Tree), *Ilex aquifolium* (Holly) and *Acer campestre* (Common Maple; also known as Hedge Maple). Climbers such as honeysuckle can be planted in soil-improved pockets near the base and encouraged to meander through the hedge. In a semi-rural area, you could use honeysuckles such as *Lonicera periclymenum* 'Belgica (Early Dutch Honeysuckle) and, especially, *Lonicera periclymenum* 'Serotina' (Late Dutch Honeysuckle) – both are described on page 30.

Clematis vitalba (Traveller's Friend; it is also more descriptively known as Old Man's Beard) is a perennial woody climber often forming a part of rural hedges. *Hedera helix* (Common Ivy) is another popular and well-known ingredient of rustic hedges.

Climbers as ground cover

Several evergreen climbers, including ivies, will cloak the ground; some have variegated leaves, others all-green foliage. They create an attractive feature, as well as helping to suppress the growth of weeds and creating an attractive background for other plants. In addition to growing vertically, the hardy and extremely robust deciduous shrub *Cotoneaster horizontalis* (Fishbone Cotoneaster) fans out horizontally (see below), and soon covers the soil.

Can climbers be used as ground cover?

IVIES AS GROUND COVER

Hedera colchica 'Sulphur Heart' has large, dominant leaves

Hedera hibernica 'Deltoidea' produces all-green leaves

Hedera colchica 'Dentata Variegata' has large leaves

Hedera helix 'Goldheart' has small, brightly coloured leaves

Ivies are resilient and adaptable climbers and several are ideal for clothing the ground as well as low and perhaps unsightly features, such as the bases of brick walls. Here are a few ivies to consider:

- *Hedera colchica* 'Sulphur Heart' (also known as 'Paddy's Pride') has deep green leaves splashed and irregularly streaked in bright yellow.
- *Hedera colchica* 'Dentata Variegata' (also known as *Hedera colchica* 'Dentata Aurea') has thick and leathery, bright green leaves with pale green and creamy-white edges.
- *Hedera helix* 'Goldheart' (also known as *Hedera helix* 'Oro di Bogliasco') has small, shiny-green leaves with yellow splashes at their centres. When growing in a shaded area the green becomes darker than normal.
- *Hedera hibernica* 'Deltoidea' (also known as *Hedera helix* 'Deltoidea') has all-green leaves with rounded lobes; in winter they become tinged with bronze. This ground-covering ivy, with its all-green leaves in summer, can be used to form a superb background for brightly leaved shrubs.

Several of the large-leaved, wall-covering ivies can also be used very effectively as ground cover.

VERSATILE COTONEASTER

Cotoneaster horizontalis (Fishbone Cotoneaster) is a hardy, deciduous shrub that looks superb when leaning against a white wall, where its small, green leaves, borne on herringbone-arranged branches, create an attractive contrast. However, it will also grow horizontally and is ideal for covering drains and manhole covers. When in a cottage or other informal garden – and planted 60–75 cm (2–2½ ft) from the edge of a gravel or cottage-type path – it will eventually clothe its edges. In autumn, it becomes smothered in small, glossy, red berries.

Cotoneaster horizontalis *(Fishbone Cotoneaster) is ideal for camouflaging unsightly drain and man-hole covers.*

Clematis as ground cover

Clematis are surprisingly adaptable, and apart from climbing over trellises some create colourful ground cover, especially for masking low tree stumps. Here are a few to consider.

- *Clematis flammula* (Fragrant Virgin's Bower): scrambling habit, with hawthorn-scented white flowers from late summer to mid-autumn.
- *Clematis x jouiniana*: non-clinging and shrub-like, with off-white to grey-blue flowers during late summer and into autumn.
- *Clematis rehderiana*: soft primrose-yellow flowers during late summer and into early autumn.
- *Clematis serratifolia*: pale greenish-yellow flowers with purple stamens in late summer and autumn.
- *Clematis tangutica*: grey-green leaves and lantern-shaped, rich yellow flowers from late summer to mid-autumn.
- *Clematis vitalba* (Old Man's Beard/Traveller's Joy): greenish-white flowers followed in autumn by masses of glistening, silky seedheads.

Small-garden climbers, wall shrubs and roses

Are there climbers for small gardens?

Many flowering and leafy climbers are suitable for small gardens, as well as wall shrubs and roses. Some can be combined in attractive associations (see pages 62–65), or planted on their own to create colour and interesting shapes. Never plant a climber that eventually will swamp your garden in large leaves, especially if positioned near to a boundary, and that, later, might trespass into a neighbour's garden. Also, disposing of leafy growth can be a problem.

Climbers for small gardens

- *Akebia quinata* (see page 24)
- *Clematis chrysocoma* (see page 26)
- *Clematis flammula* (see page 26)
- *Clematis florida* 'Sieboldiana' (see page 26)
- *Clematis* 'Frances Rivis' (see page 26)
- *Clematis macropetala* (see page 27)
- *Clematis* 'Marie Boisselot' (see page 27)
- *Clematis* 'Mrs Cholmondeley' (see page 27)
- *Clematis* 'Nelly Moser' (see page 27)
- *Clematis orientalis* (see page 27)
- *Clematis tangutica* (see page 28)
- *Clematis* 'Ville de Lyon' (see page 28)
- *Lapageria rosea* (see page 29)
- *Lonicera periclymenum* 'Belgica' (see page 30)
- *Lonicera periclymenum* 'Serotina' (see page 30)
- *Passiflora caerulea* (see page 30)

Clematis macropetala

Wall shrubs for small gardens

- *Abeliophyllum distichum* (see page 24)
- *Abutilon megapotamicum* (see page 24)
- *Azara microphylla* (see page 25)
- *Berberidopsis corallina* (see page 25)
- *Carpenteria californica* (see page 25)
- *Ceanothus cuneatus* var. *rigidus* (see page 25)
- *Ceanothus thyrsiflorus* var. *repens* (see page 25)
- *Chimonanthus praecox* (see page 26)
- *Fremontodendron californicum* (see page 28)
- *Garrya elliptica* (see page 29)
- *Jasminum nudiflorum* (see page 29)
- *Trachelospermum jasminoides* (see page 31)

Carpenteria californica

CLIMBING ANNUALS

Several of these floriferous climbers are suitable for small gardens (see pages 32–33).
- *Caiophora laterita* 'Frothy'
- *Ipomoea purpurea*
- *Ipomoea tricolor* 'Heavenly Blue'
- *Lathyrus odoratus*
- *Lophospermum scandens* 'Jewel Mixed'
- *Maurandella antirrhiniflora* 'Mixed'
- *Thunbergia alata*
- *Tropaeolum majus*

Climbing and rambling roses for small gardens

- 'Adélaïde d'Orléans' (see page 40)
- 'Aimée Vibert' (see page 40)
- 'Alister Stella Gray' (see page 41)
- 'Aloha' (see page 41)
- 'Climbing Crimson Glory' (see page 42)
- 'Climbing Lady Sylvia' (see page 42)
- 'Climbing Lady Hillingdon' (see page 42)
- 'Constance Spry' (see page 42)
- 'Crimson Shower' (see page 42)
- 'Danse du Feu' (see page 43)
- 'Gerbe Rose' (see page 43)
- 'Golden Showers' (see page 43)
- 'Kathleen Harrop' (see page 44)
- 'Leverkusen' (see page 44)
- 'Maigold' (see page 44)
- 'New Dawn' (see page 45)
- 'Pink Perpétué' (see page 45)
- 'Rêve d'Or' (see page 46)
- 'Shropshire Lass' (see page 46)
- 'St Swithun' (see page 46)
- 'Zéphirine Drouhin' (see page 47)

Note: these roses range in height from 2.4 to 4.5 m (8–15 ft).

Constance Spry

Colour parade

A wide spectrum of flower colours is displayed by climbers, wall shrubs and both climbing and rambling roses, ranging from white, through yellow, red and pink, blue and purple to those with mixed colours. Here are at-a-glance suggestions for plants producing these colours, making the selection of plants quick and easy. Climbers with attractive leaves are paraded on pages 34–35, while those with rich autumn colours are shown on pages 36–37.

What is the range of colours?

FLOWER COLOUR GROUPS

WHITE	YELLOW	RED AND PINK	BLUE AND PURPLE	MIXED COLOURS
Climbers	**Climbers**	**Climbers**	**Climbers**	**Climbers**
• *Clematis armandii* (see page 26)	• *Clematis orientalis* (see page 27)	• *Clematis* 'Ville de Lyon' (see page 28)	• *Clematis* 'Frances Rivis' (see page 26)	• *Clematis florida* 'Sieboldiana' (see page 26)
• *Clematis chrysocoma* (see page 26)	• *Clematis rehderiana* (see page 28)	• *Eccremocarpus scaber* (see page 32)	• *Clematis macropetala* (see page 27)	• *Clematis* 'Nelly Moser' (see page 27)
• *Clematis flammula* (see page 26)	• *Clematis tangutica* (see page 28)	• *Lapageria rosea* (see page 29)	• *Clematis* 'Mrs Cholmondeley' (see page 27)	• *Lonicera periclymenum* 'Belgica' (see page 30)
• *Clematis* 'Marie Boisselot' (see page 27)	• *Lonicera tragophylla* (see page 30)		• *Cobaea scandens* (see page 32)	• *Lonicera periclymenum* 'Serotina' (see page 30)
• *Clematis montana* (see page 27)		**Wall shrubs**	• *Ipomoea purpurea* (see page 32)	• *Passiflora caerulea* (see page 30)
• *Fallopia baldschuanica* (see page 28)	**Wall shrubs**	• *Berberidopsis corallina* (see page 25)	• *Ipomoea tricolor* 'Heavenly Blue' (see page 32)	
• *Hydrangea anomala* subsp. *petiolaris* (see page 29)	• *Azara microphylla* (see page 25)		• *Solanum crispum* (see page 30)	**Wall shrubs**
• *Jasminum officinale* (see page 29)	• *Cytisus battandieri* (see page 28)	**Roses**	• *Wisteria floribunda* (see page 31)	• *Abutilon megapotamicum* (see page 24)
• *Trachelospermum jasminoides* (see page 31)	• *Fremontodendron californicum* (see page 28)	• 'Albertine' (see page 41)	• *Wisteria sinensis* (see page 31)	• *Chimonanthus praecox* (see page 26)
	• *Jasminum nudiflorum* (see page 29)	• 'Alexander Girault' (see page 41)		
Wall shrubs		• 'Aloha' (see page 41)	**Wall shrubs**	
• *Abeliophyllum distichum* (see page 24)	**Roses**	• 'Climbing Cécile Brunner' (see page 41)	• *Ceanothus cuneatus* var. *rigidus* (see page 25)	
• *Carpenteria californica* (see page 25)	• 'Alister Stella Gray' (see page 41)	• 'Climbing Crimson Glory' (see page 42)	• *Ceanothus thyrsiflorus* var. *repens* (see page 25)	
	• 'Climbing Lady Hillingdon' (see page 42)	• 'Climbing Étoile de Hollande' (see page 42)	• *Solanum laxum* (see page 30)	
Roses	• 'Gloire de Dijon' (see page 43)	• 'Climbing Lady Sylvia' (see page 42)		
• 'Aimée Vibert' (see page 40)	• 'Golden Showers' (see page 43)	• 'Constance Spry' (see page 42)		
• 'Albéric Barbier' (see page 40)	• 'Leverkusen' (see page 44)	• 'Crimson Shower' (see page 42)		
• 'Bobbie James' (see page 41)	• 'Maigold' (see page 44)	• 'François Juranville' (see page 43)		
• 'Madame Alfred Carrière' (see page 44)	• 'Mermaid' (see page 45)	• 'Guinée' (see page 43)		
• 'Rambling Rector' (see page 46)		• 'New Dawn' (see page 45)		
• 'Sander's White Rambler' (see page 46)		• 'Zéphirine Drouhin' (see page 47)		
• 'Wedding Day' (see page 47)				

Rose colours

The colours of roses often vary and are frequently open to interpretation. Colours fade, while the time of day and intensity of light encourage different impressions. We all have our own ideas of colours, especially when shades merge one with another. Therefore, use the above colours solely as a guide.

Problems with climbers

Are climbers affected by pests and diseases?

Few climbers and wall shrubs escape the ravages of pests and diseases, but woody and perennial types are least susceptible. Annual climbers are especially vulnerable to slugs and snails, as well as aphids and caterpillars. Climbing and rambling roses are also prey to pests and diseases; some, such as black spot, are notorious to roses. Honeysuckles do not escape either, with aphids causing damage to both flowers and tender shoots.

Aphids (greenfly)

Aphids (greenfly) suck sap, causing mottling and distortion. They also transmit viruses from plant to plant and tend to congregate under leaves and around leaf-joints. As soon as aphids are seen, spray the plants. Young and tender annuals, as well as herbaceous climbers, are especially vulnerable to aphids.

Black spot

Black spot is a fungal disease of roses, causing unsightly black spots on leaves. When the disease is severe, the spots merge to form large, blackened areas. It is the young leaves that are first infected. As soon as the disease is seen, spray the leaves with a fungicide. Also remove and burn fallen, infected leaves to prevent the disease spreading.

Caterpillars

Caterpillars are the larvae of moths and butterflies. They infest garden plants, eating and chewing their way through soft stems, flowers and leaves. The adults are harmless in themselves and gardeners often delight in seeing them. Pick off small clusters of caterpillars. Alternatively, spray with a proprietary insecticide as soon as they – or the damage – are seen.

Cockchafer beetles

Cockchafer beetles are also known as 'May bugs' and 'June bugs', and both adult beetles and larvae attack plants. Adult beetles feed and fly during early and mid-summer, chewing flowers and leaves. The dirty, creamy-white larvae are about 30 mm (1¼ in) long and are usually curled up. They live in the soil and chew roots. Whenever possible, pick up and destroy larvae when digging and preparing the soil. Additionally, dust leaves with an insecticide.

Cuckoo spit

Cuckoo spit, a white and frothy spittle that encloses insects called froghoppers, is an eyesore. Froghoppers attack a wide range of garden plants, causing leaves to become distorted. They are more prevalent in late spring and early summer, the young nymphs being responsible for most of the damage. They produce the cuckoo spit to protect themselves against birds and other predators. Spray them either with a strong jet of water, or with an insecticide.

Earwigs

Earwigs are pernicious and omnipresent pests. They clamber into plants, damaging soft stems, leaves and flowers. They especially like dark and secluded areas, perhaps between plants and walls. Pick them off and destroy them. Also trap them in pots filled with straw and inverted on the tops of bamboo canes. Each morning, empty and destroy the earwigs. Additionally, spray or dust with a pesticide.

Leafhoppers

Leafhoppers, which are related to greenfly, create pale, mottled areas on leaves, especially those on roses. Growth becomes checked and leaves distorted; they may even fall off if the attack is severe, especially in dry weather. The young leafhoppers feed on the undersides of leaves and jump and fly off when disturbed. As well as disfiguring plants, they transmit viruses. Spray with a systemic insecticide.

Red spider mites

Red spider mites cause bronzed patches on the upper surfaces of leaves and fine webbing on the undersides. In a wall shrub garden they are most likely to be found on fruit trees, such as apples and pears. The mites are minute, rusty-red and with four pairs of legs and only just visible under a hand lens. Damp and wet weather reduces their spread. Spray plants several times in summer, using a suitable chemical.

Rose rust

Rose rust is quite common and difficult to eradicate. It is an unsightly disease, with orange swellings on the undersides of leaves. In late summer, they turn black. New shoots become reddish and shrivel. Spray plants regularly, especially if it is a widespread problem in your area. Feeding plants with a balanced fertilizer in early summer also helps keep plants healthy.

Rose scale

Rose scale is most often seen on old and neglected roses, appearing as scurfy scales clustered on stems. The scale weakens plants, making them even more unsightly. When the infection is only slight, wipe off colonies using methylated spirits (rubbing alcohol). Alternatively, use a systemic insecticide. If infection is severe, cut out infected stems and burn them.

Slugs

Slugs are destructive and soon decimate plants, especially those with soft stems and leaves. They are most troublesome during wet and warm weather, when they chew leaves, stems and shoots. They mainly feed at night and therefore are not always seen. Use slug baits, but ensure they are not accessible to family pets and wildlife.

Snails

Snails, like slugs, are pests of the night, especially during warm and wet weather. They chew and tear leaves and stems. Pick off and destroy them as soon as they are seen. Also use baits in the same way as when trapping and killing slugs. After a shower of rain, snails often appear in large numbers.

CLEMATIS WILT DISEASE

This pernicious disease, occasionally known as dieback, is especially troublesome on large-flowered hybrid-type clematis, and although it is a widespread problem there is no really reliable cure. Species and small-flowered hybrids are not so likely to be infected. Additionally, plants growing on their own roots are often less susceptible than grafted ones.

Affected plants suddenly wilt for no apparent reason, with the problem starting just above or slightly below soil level. Wilted plants seldom recover, but young shoots sometimes arise below the wilted area. Cut out wilted shoots and, in spring, spray with a fungicide. Also feed plants to encourage fresh growth.

Clematis 'Nelly Moser', a popular and widely grown large-flowered clematis, is sometimes troubled by clematis wilt, a disease that is also known as 'dieback'.

Glossary

Acid soil Soil which has a pH of less than 7.0 (see pH).

Alkaline soil Soil which has a pH above 7.0 (see pH).

Annual A plant that grows from seed, flowers and dies within the same year. However, many plants that are not strictly annuals are treated as such. For example, *Tropaeolum peregrinum* (Canary Creeper) is a half-hardy, short-lived perennial usually grown as a hardy annual; *Cobaea scandens* (Cathedral Bells) is a half-hardy perennial usually grown as a half-hardy annual; *Caiophora laterita* 'Frothy' is a biennial or short-lived perennial usually grown as a half-hardy annual.

Anvil secateurs Type of secateurs, where a blade cuts against a firm, metal surface.

Biennial Plants with a two-year growing cycle and raised from seeds sown during one year for flowering in the following one.

Bud A tightly packed and closed immature shoot or flower.

Bypass secateurs Type of secateurs where one blade crosses the other. Earlier known as parrot-type and cross-over secateurs.

Climber A plant – whether woody, herbaceous or with an annual growth cycle – that has a natural tendency to climb. Their growth cycles are described on page 3 and climbing characteristics on page 12.

Climbing rose These have larger flowers than rambling types, and are borne single or in small groups and with the ability to repeat flowering after their first period of bloom.

Container-grown plant A way in which plants are sometimes sold. Plants established and growing in a container may be evergreen or deciduous climbers, wall shrubs, shrubs or trees, or herbaceous perennials or rock-garden plants. They can be planted at any time of the year when the soil and weather are suitable.

Cordon A fruit tree (usually an apple or pear tree), although it can be a soft fruit such as a red- or whitecurrant, that is trained and pruned to form one, two, three or four stems. Mostly, they are grown at a 45° angle, although some are upright.

Cultivar A variety raised in cultivation, rather than appearing naturally without any interference from humans. Properly, the vast majority of varieties should be known as cultivars, but 'variety' is the better-known term and is often seen in books, as well as being used in conversation.

Deciduous Describes shrubs and trees, as well as climbers and wall shrubs and some conifers, that shed their leaves in autumn and produce a fresh array in spring. A few slightly tender evergreens lose some of their leaves during cold weather.

Espalier A fruit tree trained so that its branches form tiers, usually supported by a framework of wires.

Evergreen Describes plants that retain their leaves throughout the year and therefore always appear green. However, they regularly lose some of their leaves, while producing further ones.

Form A loose and rather non-botanical term used to refer to a variation within a particular species.

Friable Refers to soil that is crumbly.

Genus A group of species with common botanical characteristics. When designating a plant, the genus name is put first (usually in italics), with an initial capital letter.

Hardening off The gradual acclimatizing of tender plants (often half-hardy annuals) to outside conditions. Garden frames are useful for this purpose.

Hardy Describes a plant that is able to survive winter outdoors in a temperate climate.

Herbaceous Describes a plant that dies down to soil level in autumn or early winter, after the completion of each season's growth. Fresh shoots appear in spring.

Layering A vegetative method of increasing plants by lowering stems and shallowly burying them in the ground. By twisting, bending or slitting the stem at the point where it is buried, the flow of sap is restricted and roots induced to form.

Loppers Long-handled secateurs, used to cut thick shoots. They have either a bypass or an anvil-cutting action.

Mulching Covering soil around plants with a thick layer of well-decomposed organic material such as garden compost or manure.

Parrot secateurs An early name for bypass or cross-over secateurs, where one blade crosses another.

Partially evergreen Describes shrubs that remain evergreen in most climates, but in cold winters may lose some or all of their leaves.

Petiole A leaf-stalk; some are adapted to give a climber support.

pH A scale from 0 to 14 that defines the alkalinity or acidity of soil. A pH of 7.0 is neutral; figures above this indicate increasing alkalinity, and those below increasing acidity.

Pillar rose Both rambling and climbing roses can be used to clothe pillars, which are usually rustic poles about 2.1 m (7 ft) high and often cut from conifers.

Pruning The controlled removal of shoots to encourage a plant to form a better or desired shape, develop fruits and flowers and, in a few instances, produce attractive stems.

Rambling roses (ramblers) These bear many large bunches of small flowers. Unfortunately, flowering is usually just for a single period in the year.

Shrub Woody plant with several stems coming from ground level. Some plants can be grown as a tree or as a shrub, depending on the initial pruning and training.

Species A botanical classification within a genus (usually written in italics with no initial capital, after the genus name). There may be one or several species within a genus.

Subsoil Soil below the normal depth at which the soil is cultivated.

Sucker A shoot which grows from a stem or root of a grafted or budded plant, below the position where the varietal part and the rootstock were united.

Synonym An alternative name for a plant (usually a superseded one).

Topsoil Top layer of soil in which most plants grow.

Tree A woody plant with a permanently clear stem between the branches and the ground.

Variegated Mainly applied to leaves and used to describe a state of having two or more colours.

Variety At one time, all variations within a species were known as varieties. Now, correctly, varieties raised in cultivation are known as cultivars.

Wall shrub A shrub that can be trained against a wall. Some wall shrubs are hardy and withstand low temperatures, while others are tender and require the comfort of a sunny wall.

Index

Acknowledgments

AG&G Books would like to thank the RHS Gardens at Hyde Hall, Rettendon, Chelmsford, Essex, England and at Wisley, Woking, Surrey, England. David Lawton's garden is featured on the front of the cover – thank you Dave. Photographs: AG&G Books (cover and pages 2, 3, 5, 12TL, BL and BR, 24C, 25BL and BR, 26TC, TR, and BL, 27TC, BC, and BL, 28BL, BC, and BL, 29TL, and TR, 30BL, 31TL, and TR, 33TL, BL, and BC, 35TL, TC, and BL, 37TR, 39TR, and BL, 41BC, 42BR, 43TL, 44TL, 45TC, TR, and BR, 46TC, TR, and BR, 47TR, 48, 50, 52, 57, 61, 68, 69 and 71), David Squire (pages 12TR, 27TL, 31TC, 35BC, and BR, 37TL, 38BL, 39TL and 73), Garden Matters (page 28TL), Garden World Images (pages 29BL, 30TL, 32BL, 33TL, 39TC, and BL, 41TR, 42TL, TC, and BR, 43BR, 45TL, BL, and BC and 46BL, and BC), Garden Picture Library (page 40BL), Harry Smith Collection (pages 25TC, 26BL, 34BL, 40BC, 41TL, 42BC, and 43TR, and BC) and Peter McHoy (pages 24BL, and BR, 25TL, TR, and TC, 26TL, and BC, 27TL, and BL, 28TC, and TL, 29TC, BC, and BL, 30TC, TR, BC, BR, BC, and BL, 33TC, and BL, 34BC, and BR, 35TR, 36, 37TC, BL, and BC, 38BL, and BC, 39BC, 40BR, 41TL, BL, and BR, 43TC, and BL, 44TL, BL, BC, and BL, 47TC and 72).